The War on Terror

The Canadian Dilemma

To Helene,

I hope you enjoy & Thank you for taking such good care of my Keith! Olivia

The War on Terror

The Canadian Dilemma

Olivier Courteaux

The War on Terror : the Canadian Dilemma, by Olivier Courteaux

Copyright © 2009 by Olivier Courteaux
Manufactured in the United States of America. All rights reserved. No part of this book may be reproduced in any form or by any means, electronic or mechanical, including photocopying, recording, or by an information storage and retrieval system – except by a reviewer who may quote brief passages in a review to be printed in a magazine, newspaper, or on the Web – without permission in writing from the publisher.

Although the author and publisher have made every effort to ensure the accuracy and completeness of information contained in this book, we assume no responsibility for errors, inaccuracies, omissions or inconsistencies herein. Any slights of people, places, or organizations are unintentional.

Published by
Hispanic Economics
P.O. Box 140681
Coral Gables, FL 33114-0681
info@hispaniceconomics.com
HispanicEconomics.com

ISBN: 978-0-9791176-1-9

Cover and Interior Design by John Clifton
johnclifton.net

Acknowledgements

A great majority of Americans know very little about their neighbour to the north, except perhaps that Canadians live in a land of ice and snow, have a passion for endlessly skating on frozen canals and tend to end their sentences with a funny "eh". But Canada does indeed enjoy warm summers. It also shares the world's longest, unmilitarized border with the United States and remains that country's number one trading partner. Who knew?

I am extremely grateful to Louis Nevaer for the opportunity to dispel some enduring clichés, particularly within the scope of the ongoing battle against global terrorism. In the immediate aftermath of the attacks against the World Trade Center and the Pentagon, some Washington pundits claimed that the terrorists who killed so many innocent people had entered the country from Canada.

As it turned out, the accusation was unfounded but stubbornly enduring. On several occasions Canadian authorities felt compelled to demand both an apology and a retraction. The most recent incident involved Janet Napolitano, the new U.S. Secretary for Homeland Security. In April 2009, she unabashedly made the same claim against Canada, provoking angry reactions in Ottawa. "Nonetheless," she maintained all along, "to the extent that terrorists have come into our country or suspected or known terrorists have entered our country across a border, it's been across the Canadian border."[1]

My sincere hope is that this modest contribution to the debate over Canada's role in the War on Terror will clarify some of those myths and provide a clearer picture of Canada's actions and intentions following 9/11.

Louis Nevaer championed this project from the start, and his unfailing support and patience are greatly appreciated.

Much is also owed to Gord McLaughlin, a superb writer and editor, who took the time to read earlier drafts of my manuscript. His advice was invaluable.

My thanks go to all those who helped me in this endeavour. A special thank you to my colleagues at Ryerson University in Toronto, Dr. Rob Teigrob and Dr. Arne Kislenko, Dr. Carl Benn, the Chair of the History Department, for their help and support, and to my former student, Jacob Ginsberg, who shared his notes with me after attending the Canadian Association for Intelligence and Security Studies 2008 International Conference. Finally my thanks to my family, my parents especially, for believing in me.

---

[1] CBCNews.ca, "Canada more lax than US about whom it lets in, Napolitano says," 21 April 2009
http://www.cbc.ca/world/story/2009/04/21/napolitano-border-canada021.html

Contents

INTRODUCTION 1

The War on Terror: The Canadian Dilemma 1

CHAPTER 1 ..... **8**

The United States Since 9/11: The Bush Administration and the "Global War" Against Terrorism 8

The Theory of the "Clash of Civilizations" and Global Terrorism 10

The Lessons of Pearl Harbor 12

The War on Terror: A Question of Legitimacy 17

The War on Terror: The Notion of Preventive Action 20

Pre-Emptive or Preventive Action? 23

Preventive Action as a Military Strategy: The Importance of Intelligence and Planning 27

The Political and Diplomatic Consequences of a Preventive Strategy 31

CHAPTER 2 ..... **35**

Canada and the War on Terror "Made in USA": Border Security and Immigration 35

"Fortress America": The USA PATRIOT Act, Homeland Security and Other Tales 37

Canada, A "Haven" for Terrorists? 41

The Case of Maher Arar 46

Sharing a Continent   50

CHAPTER 3   **56**

Canada's Contribution to the War on Terror 2001-2003:
Canada, America's Best Friend?   56

Security: The New Priority   58

Canada: A Peacekeeping Nation?   63

Canada-US Defense Relations: The Ballistic Missile Defense   72

The Afghan Mission: Operation "Enduring Freedom" and
Beyond   75

Iraq: The Big Divide   79

CHAPTER 4   **83**

Canada's Security Dilemma: How to Manage the Reaction
to the American Reaction   83

Securing an Open Society: A New Era for Security Issues in
Canada   85

Canada's "Three Core National Security Interests"   91

The Ballistic Missile Defense (BMD) Initiative... Again!   100

The Afghan Challenge: Canada's Mission to End in 2011?   106

CONCLUSION   **115**
NOTES   122
SELECTED SECONDARY SOURCES   133
INDEX   137

Introduction

The War on Terror: The Canadian Dilemma

On the morning of September 12, 2001, the bold banner headline in the French daily *Le Monde* — We Are All Americans — fairly summed up the prevailing mood in much of the world. The destruction of the World Trade Center was greeted with shock, disbelief and widespread condemnation. In rare solidarity, the United Nations, NATO, the European Union and, in their wake, an impressive number of governments strongly denounced the deadly attacks and offered their unambiguous support in the struggle against international terrorism. Jean Chrétien, the Canadian Prime Minister, said in a statement: "there can be no cause or grievance that could justify such unspeakable violence. Indeed, such an attack is an assault not only on the targets but an offence against the freedom and rights of all civilized nations."[1]

"Sept. 11, 2001, ushers in a new age,"[2] noted *Le Monde*. "It is a different world [...] It's a new kind of threat,"[3] argued Colin Powell, then U.S. Secretary of State. In a matter of a few hours, terrorism was established as an unparalleled threat to post-cold war stability. At stake were the fundamental values of democracy and freedom. Exceptional in nature, or so was the new perception, terrorism forced America and its close allies to consider exceptional measures — political, diplomatic, military and judiciary - to effectively fight those enemies who "reject basic human values and hate the United States and everything for which it stands."[4] It was as if an epoch of peace and confidence had suddenly faded, and a new era of uncertainty had taken its place. In wiping out so many innocent lives, terrorism suddenly irrupted into western society as an urgent international threat, a more-than-worthy successor to the Soviet menace of decades past.

The word terrorism has been widely used over time, yet its meaning has never been precisely established. Judging by the dozens of existing definitions of so controversial a word — the United Nations actually counted 142 — it is unlikely the international community will agree on a comprehensive definition any time soon. The ambiguity of the word can be traced back to its origin. Terrorism comes from the word "terror," derived from *terrere* in Latin. Terror designates a period of the French Revolution and the attempt by the French government to annihilate all internal and external resistance to revolutionary ideas. The regime's main purpose was therefore to govern by fear. "Terror is nothing other than justice, prompt, severe, inflexible; it is therefore an emanation of virtue; it is not so much a special principle as it is a consequence of the general principle of democracy applied to our country's most urgent needs."[5] While retaining some of its initial characteristics, the notion of terrorism has evolved to take on an entirely new meaning. A terrorist act is now largely understood as political violence and subversion *against* the State, not emanating from it; to quote German sociologist Max Weber, from the French revolution on, the state "successfully [claimed] the monopoly of the legitimate use of physical force within a given territory" and the "sole source of the 'right' to use violence."[6] In other words, only the State should be in a position to impose upon society its rules of law, relying on a vast array of police, judiciary and military methods of coercion. Over time, only the state came to designate who was a terrorist and who was not.

The increasing number of terrorist acts can lead us to believe terrorism is a fairly new phenomenon. History tells us otherwise; terrorism is an ancient form of political violence that transcends geography, cultures and religions. Among the earliest exemplars were the Zealots, a Jewish political movement from the first century CE, based in the Middle-East. Its members targeted Roman dignitaries and their sympathizers as they sought to put an end to Roman occupation. Terrorist acts are a response to a strategic necessity — the need to reach pre-determined political objectives by striking an opponent that is overwhelmingly more powerful. But the various manifestations of violence as a political weapon make it all the more difficult to pinpoint precisely what the term "terrorist" means. For instance, the members of the French resistance, looked upon by the German occupants as nothing more than terrorists and criminals, have become national heroes since the end of World War II. Nelson Mandela, the anti-apartheid activist and former leader of the African National Congress, who spend twenty years in prison for terrorist crimes, later won the presidency of South Africa and the Nobel Peace prize. The perpetrators of violent acts rarely see themselves as "terrorists." The soldiers of the Irish Republican Army believed they were fighting within the framework of a war of national liberation. The 19th century Anarchists targeted the ruling classes to help a new social order settle. To the wife of the Spanish Prime Minister he had just shot to death who cried "Murderer! Assassin!," the young Italian Anarchist said: "I am not an assassin. I am the Avenger of my Anarchist comrades. I have nothing to do with you, Madame."[7]

Difficult though it may be to agree on a definition of "terrorism," political acts of violence invariably lead to a series of reactions from the State. They have evolved over time to mirror new terrorist methods, thus inaugurating a terrible cycle of retaliation and revenge. From well known individuals targeted for their political connections with a regime — the 1984 assassination of Indira Gandhi, the Indian Prime Minister, by Sikhs extremists — the acts of violence shifted to highly symbolic locations, such as the World Trade Center and the Pentagon in 2001. Then, in Madrid, in 2004, and London, in 2005, the attacks were aimed directly against ordinary civilians, used as bargaining tools to instill maximum fear and put pressure on governments. But perhaps what defines best terrorism in the later part of the 20th century is the fact it has emerged as a transnational phenomenon, a globalized threat. The terrorist methods have always included a careful choice of the targets; only, in this "global village" of ours, the propagation in real time and everywhere of sounds and images has made that choice even more crucial: the greater exposure to the media, the better. Osama Bin Laden is said to have declared that "the Western media establishment [...] implants fear and helplessness in the psyche of the people of Europe and the United States."[8] Whether he was right on this point or not is a matter of debate. But there is no denying he has repeatedly taken advantage of our age of mass media. In truth, there would be nothing more frustrating for a terrorist than to be ignored. Acts of political violence need to be acknowledged, which, in turn, requires visibility. More than a mere tool to achieve the necessary level of visibility, the Internet has allowed the terrorists to share information, coordinate and plan their actions, far from their bases of operation.

The answer to such a phenomenon appeared simple enough in the aftermath of September 11, 2001: a concerted and international response. The notion of a War on Terror was born. To fight the problem effectively, democratic states have sought to criminalize terrorism, its manifestations and its authors. They successfully managed to delegitimize acts of political violence by labeling the perpetrators as "terrorists," without making much effort to reflect upon their causes, thereby refusing to differentiate them. New York, Bali, Casablanca, Madrid, Beslan, what do they have in common? Are they all targets of Islamist fundamentalists, of a world conspiracy? Hardly so... The attack against a school in Beslan, in 2004, albeit carried out by Muslim commandos, must be placed within its unique historical and geopolitical context, that of a long standing opposition to Russian military presence in the region. The increased number of suicide attacks against Israel should be analyzed within the sole context of the Israeli-Palestinian conflict. As for the ongoing war in Iraq, the targets appear diverse: military, humanitarians, civilians and foreigners. The

Iraqi "terrorism" is a fighting strategy aimed against the presence of foreigners in the country, including the armed forces, as well as focusing on the political process imposed by the occupying power, the United States.

In the wake of the attacks against the United States in 2001, Madrid in 2004 and London in 2005, fighting terrorism efficiently without sacrificing individual freedoms remains at the centre of political debate among the Western democracies. Two notions are driving the struggle against global terrorism: counter-terrorism and anti-terrorism. "The first notion refers to the offensive measures, techniques or strategies governments adopt to prevent, deter, preempt, and respond to [terrorist attacks]."[9] Anti-terrorism, defensive in nature, encompasses the "measures used to reduce the vulnerability of individuals and property to terrorist acts."[10]

In the United States, the War on Terror orchestrated by the Bush Administration led to a wide range of anti-terrorist and counter-terrorist measures which had the effect of curtailing individual freedoms (the Patriot Act, the Department of Homeland Security). With the American intervention in Afghanistan and in Iraq, the fight was intensified beyond the boundaries of the United States (Guantanamo Bay, torture, secret prisons, etc.) Some of America's traditional allies followed suit, some were more cautious in their support. The second group included Canada. But eventually, the anti-terrorist dynamic spread within democracies and forced them to reflect on a dilemma:

how to guarantee basic human freedoms while preventing other terrorist attacks.

Canada, often considered by its southern neighbor as a weak link in the global fight against terror, adopted tough new anti-terrorism measures, the most important one being the Anti-Terrorism Act in December 2001. Canada's close ties with the United States have presented the country with very specific challenges. By advocating tougher anti-terrorist laws at home and abroad, as well as greater international cooperation against terrorism, and despite tremendous pressure from Washington, Canada has not merely been following the American model. For the most part, it has managed to maintain a balance between fighting a War on Terror and maintaining basic individual freedoms. But that fragile and far from perfect balance has come with a cost.

Chapter 1

The United States Since 9/11: The Bush Administration and the "Global War" Against Terrorism

To understand Canada's role in the War on Terror, one must first carefully examine the U.S.'s role in leading that war. In the days following the attacks on the World Trade Center and the Pentagon, it was difficult to ignore the sound of beating drums that emanated from Washington.

On September 20, 2001, U.S. President George W. Bush spoke of a "monumental fight of Good vs. Evil," declaring a "war" against terrorism. "Our War on Terror begins with al-Qaeda, but it does not end there. It will not end until every terrorist group of global reach has been found, stopped and defeated," he told a joint session of Congress. "Every nation, in every region, now has a decision to make. Either you are with us, or you are with the terrorists […] This is not, however, just America's fight. This is the world's fight. This is civilization's fight."[11] The Bush administration presented "terrorism" as an unprecedented global threat, justifying a global response.

"If a terrorist can attack at any time, in any place, and using any technique, and it's physically impossible to defend in every place, at every time against every technique, then one needs to calibrate the definition of 'defensive',"[12] declared Donald Rumsfeld, then U.S. Secretary of Defense, at a NATO conference in 2002. Afghanistan and Iraq would soon bear the brunt of America's new far-reaching and elastic philosophy.

Strikes against terrorism were nothing new, and previous administrations had already highlighted its danger. Global terrorism first became a priority for U.S. national security policy makers in 1972, following the spectacular attacks against Israeli athletes at the Munich Olympic Games. But it was more than a decade before the U.S. resorted to serious retaliation against terrorists. In 1986, President Ronald Reagan authorized air strikes against Libya in response to the bombing of a West Berlin nightclub. In 1998, President Bill Clinton ordered the launch of military strikes against terrorist facilities and infrastructure in Afghanistan and in Sudan. "Our battle against terrorism did not begin with the bombing of our embassies in Africa, nor will it end with today's strike," Clinton declared on national television. "It will require strength, courage and endurance. We will not yield to this threat. We will meet it no matter how long it may take. This will be a long, ongoing struggle between freedom and fanaticism, between the rule of law and terrorism."[13]

However, for all the ominous rhetoric, these military strikes must be seen as few and measured, certainly limited in scope and endurance. That all changed after 9/11, starting with the large-scale U.S. retaliation against Afghanistan in 2001, and then again with the broadening of the War on Terror against the regime of Saddam Hussein, who was accused of harbouring terrorists, as well as "weapons of mass destruction." The threshold for retaliating against presumed terrorist strongholds had been lowered, both strategically and symbolically. For the Bush administration, it was also clear America had to be respected in the world and recognized for what it had always been: a role model when it comes to defending and spreading democratic values and the rights of individuals.

The Theory of the "Clash of Civilizations" and Global Terrorism

In his controversial book *Clash of Civilizations*, published in 1993 in the wake of the Soviet collapse, American political scientist Samuel Huntington posited that the world has entered a period of religious conflicts between the major civilizations. He warned of growing tensions between the West and the Muslim world.

On an academic level, Huntington's theory appears simplistic and dangerous because he has done nothing to dispel existing suspicions, misconceptions and misunderstandings between the two societies. In 2005 and 2006, the Prime Ministers of Spain and Turkey proposed an international forum, the Alliance of Civilizations, under the auspices of UN Secretary-General Kofi Annan, "to improve understanding and cooperative relations among nations and peoples across cultures and religions and, in the process, to help counter the forces that fuel polarization and extremism."[14] The final 2006 report contended that cultural tensions had spread far beyond the political sphere, poisoning the minds of populations by creating dangerous stereotypes and fuelling intolerance.

This is not to ignore the real conflicts that have marked the relationship between the Muslim world and Western societies throughout history, caused by many factors: access to oil resources, which has shaped Western foreign policy in the Middle East; globalization; the Soviet invasion of Afghanistan in 1979 and the CIA's support to Islamist pro-Afghan militants; the Palestinian question and Washington's staunch support of Israel; and of course, terrorism. That is fertile ground for spreading fear and misconceptions between cultures. Media coverage of terrorist acts plays a significant role in reinforcing this idea of *us against them*.

However, a serious analysis of global terrorism over the last 20 years contradicts the thesis of a clash of civilizations. The first point worth mentioning is the great diversity of Islamist terrorism — Hamas, al-Qaeda or Hezbollah, to name just three — each with their own objectives. Second point, the undemocratic nature of most Arab regimes, unable to evolve toward multi-party societies, has fuelled deep frustrations and paved the way for radical movements. Third, the overwhelming superiority of the West in all domains generates resentment, particularly against the United States, perceived as the main beneficiary of globalization. In other words, Islamist terrorism is not the radical representation of a socio-political ensemble, the Muslim world; it is a complex phenomenon that encompasses several forces: religion, of course; globalization, seen as a vector of change and uniformity; oil; and political and economic frustrations. Unfortunately, simplistic theories such as the emergence of a "clash of civilizations" — and the attendant misconceptions between cultures — appear to have been a cornerstone of the post-9/11 Bush Doctrine.

The Lessons of Pearl Harbor

The Bush administration's immediate response to the attacks on September 11 borrowed heavily from history, with echoes from World War II, the American "Wild West" and, according to some critics, even the Middle Ages. Historical references helped to validate the idea of a War on Terror, beginning with Japan's surprise attack against Pearl Harbor, on December 7, 1941. That "day of infamy," to quote Franklin Roosevelt's famous speech, galvanized and united a traumatized nation. Never before had the United States been attacked on its own soil. The American secret service had failed to anticipate the operation despite ominous warnings.

Yet, the attacks on 9/11 bore little resemblance to Pearl Harbor. In 2001, the world was not at war and, more importantly, the enemy was not a hostile foreign state. The targets were not only military (the Pentagon), they were also, and above all, civilian. The twin towers were economic symbols, the workplace of thousands of people representing more than 40 nationalities among the civilian casualties. Regardless of these discrepancies, the Bush administration invoked Pearl Harbor with good reason. Pearl Harbor created an immediate state of war against two of the most notorious totalitarian regimes of the day, Japan and Nazi Germany. Their total surrender in 1945, led to the introduction of the nuclear bombs (Hiroshima and Nagasaki) and the first international trial for war crimes and crimes against humanity.

In that sense, the repeated references to Pearl Harbor psychologically prepared a shocked American public for the idea of another war against another stealthy invader. From the crushing blow that was Pearl Harbor came victory and the rise of the U.S. as a world superpower. The message of the Bush administration was that the 9/11 terrorists would not prevail, just as the Japanese had been vanquished during World War II, and that America would once more emerge as the heroic foe of tyranny.

"After all that has just passed — all the lives taken, and all the possibilities and hopes that died with them — it is natural to wonder if America's future is one of fear," declared President Bush. "Some speak of an age of terror. I know there are struggles ahead, and dangers to face. But this country will define our times, not be defined by them. As long as the United States of America is determined and strong, this will not be an age of terror; this will be an age of liberty, here and across the world."[15]

George W. Bush evoked an older, more mythical chapter of U.S. history when he addressed the American people on September 17, 2001. He vowed that those responsible for the 9/11 attacks would be caught "dead or alive."[16] The American public applauded the familiar and comforting slogan. It hearkened back to the Wild West frontier, when criminals were pursued until they were caught, judged and hanged. This powerful metaphor and other frontier symbols should not be underestimated.

In March 1983, then-U.S. President Ronald Reagan agreed to open an exhibition organized by the Library of Congress entitled "The American Cowboy." Considering his past career as a Western film star, it was hardly surprising that he would take part. Since his inauguration two years earlier, Reagan had espoused the belief that Americans should return to those values associated with America's frontier heritage: individualism, self-reliance and democratic integrity. "If we understand this part of our history, we will better understand how our people see themselves and the hopes they have for America," he said.[17] Americans have come to regard the conquest of the West as a defining moment in their history, and George W. Bush understood this.

But did he understand the implications when he called for a "crusade against evil"? His use of the word "crusade" shocked many pundits. Was George W. Bush referring to the medieval crusades against the Muslims? And if so, what would make his crusade against terrorism so different from the Islamic *Jihad*? By trumpeting the War on Terror as "the world's fight," and "civilization's fight," was the American president too arrogant?

In truth, Bush was likely not invoking the medieval crusades but a more contemporary world vision shared by many of his predecessors. For instance, Woodrow Wilson's 1917 crusade for freedom of commerce on the high seas and a new world order based on democratic principles. Or Dwight Eisenhower who named his memoirs "Crusade for Europe." Or Ronald Reagan who, in 1983, made public his intention to fight "the Empire of Evil," namely the Soviet Union.

In many ways, George W. Bush did nothing but praise his country's uniqueness, the sense of Manifest Destiny that predominates in the American psyche. Born out of revolution, the United States has always considered itself an exceptional country of citizens unified by their allegiance to a common set of democratic ideals. These assumptions and terms of reference can be traced back to the first Puritan migrants and their endeavour to make the New World a haven for the oppressed. Exceptionalism describes the perception of those early colonists who, as Pilgrims, were charged with a spiritual and political destiny: to create in the New World a church and a society that would provide the model for all the nations of Europe. The New World was considered the last and best chance offered by God to a fallen humanity that had only to look to this new church for redemption. Thus, America and Americans are exceptional because they are charged with saving the world from itself. At the same time, America and Americans must sustain a high level of spiritual, political and moral commitment to be worthy of this exceptional destiny — America must be "a city upon a hill" exposed to the eyes of the world.

In his inaugural address (April 1789), George Washington declared: "No people can be bound to acknowledge and adore the Invisible Hand which conducts the affairs of men more than those of the United States. Every step by which they have advanced to the character of an independent nation seems to have been distinguished by some token of providential agency."[18] From Washington to Bush, no U.S. president ever has faltered by declaring that God was on his nation's side.

The political discourse on American exceptionalism has not changed much since George Washington's address. "The United States possesses unprecedented — and unequalled — strength and influence in the world," declared Bush in a June 2002 speech delivered at West Point. "Sustained by faith in the principles of liberty, and the value of a free society, this position comes with unparalleled responsibilities, obligations, and opportunity."[19] America's universal mission, as understood and accepted by a great majority of Americans, helps to explain their shock and disbelief following the 9/11 attacks. "Americans are asking: why do they hate us? They hate what we see right here in this chamber — a democratically elected government. Their leaders are self-appointed. They hate our freedoms — our freedom of religion, our freedom of speech, our freedom to vote and assemble and disagree with each other." Bush proclaimed that the United States epitomizes universal ideals of freedom and democracy, so that any attack on American soil is an attack against all "civilized" nations. And as long as the world's democracies agree on such a threat, they must consolidate their common ideals and offer a military response to crush the new enemies, at the source, wherever that may be. Once the American public accepted the idea of a global War on Terror, the U.S. could wage actual wars on specific countries with little domestic backlash.

The War on Terror: A Question of Legitimacy

Following the September 11 attacks, members of the North Atlantic Treaty Organization (NATO) swiftly invoked, for the first time in the organization's history, article 5 of its charter: "The Parties agree that an armed attack against one or more of them in Europe or North America shall be considered an attack against them all." Meanwhile, the United Nations Security Council adopted resolution 1368, which not only condemned "in the strongest terms the horrifying terrorist attacks" deemed "a threat to international peace and security," but recognized "the inherent right of individual or collective self-defense in accordance with the Charter."

On November 12, the UN went even further by adopting resolution 1377; it declared "that acts of international terrorism constitute one of the most serious threats to international peace and security in the twenty-first century." In the process the Security Council called for "a sustained, comprehensive approach involving the active participation of all Member States of the United Nations" in accordance with Chapter VII of the Charter. In principle, the Security Council alone has the authority to take the appropriate measures against "the existence of any threat to the peace," but a member state can always invoke two exceptions to that international rule of law: self-defense (Article 51) and threat to peace and international security.

The Bush administration chose self-defense to validate its first military action in this newly declared War on Terror. This came on the heels of a British government report, released on October 4, 2001, that revealed ties between al-Qaeda and Afghanistan's rulers, the Taliban.[20] On October 7, 2001 the United States notified the UN Security Council it was launching Operation Enduring Freedom against Afghanistan, in compliance with Article 51. In its initial stage, the operation was a powerful mix of air strikes and deployment of at least 1,000 troops, including Special Forces. The objectives were clear: to destroy terrorist training camps within Afghanistan and capturing al-Qaeda's leaders. Within two months, the Taliban regime had collapsed. But as it turned out, the war against terrorism was not yet over.

On January 29, 2002, in his State of the Union address, George Bush declared: "Our discoveries in Afghanistan confirmed our worst fears, and showed us the true scope of the task ahead […] What we have found in Afghanistan confirms that, far from ending there, our war against terror is only beginning […] Our second goal is to prevent regimes that sponsor terror from threatening America or our friends and allies with weapons of mass destruction. Some of these regimes have been pretty quiet since September the 11th. But we know their true nature. North Korea is a regime arming with missiles and weapons of mass destruction, while starving its citizens. Iran aggressively pursues these weapons and exports terror, while an unelected few repress the Iranian people's hope for freedom. Iraq continues to flaunt its hostility toward America and to support terror."[21]

Bush's rhetoric against "rogue states" and an "axis of evil" echoed neo-conservative doctrine established in the 1990s: more than ever, America had to defend and and export democratic values to make the world safer.

The Bush administration also used the concept of humanitarianism to justify its interventions — against the oppressive Taliban in Afghanistan and tyrannical Saddam Hussein in Iraq. This ignored the fact that it was the U.S. — through its Central Intelligence Agency — that first armed the Taliban back in the 1980s. This had been done to help fight off invading Soviet forces, which spent a decade trying to conquer the desolate country. Following the Soviet withdrawal of 1989, the Taliban won the Afghan civil war and imposed its own repressive regime. Therefore, the Bush administration could portray its invasion as more than just retaliation for the September 11 attacks, it was also hailed as a humanitarian intervention. "Afghanistan has been liberated," boasted Bush.

In the end, no matter the justification for war, the attacks on September 11 helped define new forms of aggressor. The enemy was no longer a state or a group of states. "Defending our Nation against its enemies is the first and fundamental commitment of the Federal government," George W. Bush declared on September

17, 2002. "Today, the task has changed dramatically. Enemies in the past needed great armies and great industrial capabilities to endanger America. Now, shadowy networks of individuals can bring great chaos and suffering to our shores for less than it costs to purchase a single tank."[22] The enemy was now transnational and non-military, and it required a new response: preventive military action

The War on Terror: The Notion of Preventive Action

As mentioned, Article 51 of the UN Charter permits self-defense, but only "until the Security Council has taken measures necessary to maintain international peace and security." In 2002, for the first time, the U. S. openly contested such a notion in the name of what was called the "Bush Doctrine." As the optimism of the 1990s came abruptly to an end on the morning of September 11, the Bush administration made the case for a new foreign policy. A year later the White House released a document entitled *The National Security Strategy of the United States of America*. As the celebrated lawyer Alan Dershowitz noted, the document "began with a discussion of deterrence as the major strategy in dealing with the Soviet Union and its allies during the Cold War."[23]

The concepts of containment and deterrence — the art of showing one's strength and will to maintain peace — were introduced by the Truman administration in 1947. They remained the favored approach to maintaining a fragile balance of power with the Soviet Union, until the collapse of the Soviet bloc in 1989. The subsequent disintegration of the Soviet Union brought an end to a complex international system based on a precarious nuclear equilibrium. The Bush Doctrine held that in the face of a growing global international threat, deterrence had become obsolete: "… the threat of retaliation is less likely to work against leaders of rogue states more willing to take risks," and who see "weapons of mass destruction as weapons of choice."[24]

The basic assumptions underlying the new foreign policy strategy were fourfold, as outlined by George Bush in his West Point speech. 1) The United States must defend peace against "terrorists and tyrants," 2) safeguard that peace by building good relations with traditional allies, and 3) spread peace on every continent by helping free and open societies. Finally, 4) the alliance between radicalism and technology is the main threat to peace. Weapons of mass destruction in the hands of terrorists or "rogue states" constitute a grave threat to the US and to other democracies. Consequently, those enemies must be neutralized, and pre-emptive strikes would help to keep them on the defensive. "We must be prepared to stop rogue states and their terrorist clients before they are able to threaten or use weapons of mass destruction against the United States and our allies and friends." The U.S. is therefore ready to act against emerging threats "to our national security."[25] Action is the only way to build a lasting peace and security.

Wolfowitz, Libby, Rumsfeld... The War in Iraq made them famous. However, their influence in drafting the new doctrine was not rooted in the attacks of 9/11 but in the aftermath of the Cold War. In 1994, Paul Wolfowitz and Lewis Libby, who became assistant secretary of defense and Vice President Dick Cheney's advisor, drafted the *Defense Policy Guidance*, a policy document that called for independent U.S. action, if necessary, to prevent any state or group of states from defying American leadership in the world. The notion of pre-emption was clearly suggested. President George H. W. Bush had kept the neo-conservatives at a safe distance, favoring a balance-of-power type of foreign policy, which culminated in the first Gulf War in 1991; however, his son proved much more amenable to "neo-con" ideas. In January 2001, Dick Cheney became vice president, Donald Rumsfeld secretary of defense and Paul Wolfowitz deputy secretary of defense. Later that year, the attacks on 9/11 made it possible for them to realize their vision. "Every nation has the right of self-defense and this is the only, only conceivable way for us to defend ourselves against those kinds of [terrorist] threats,"[26] declared Rumsfeld at a NATO conference in 2002. In order words, the ban on the use of military force as established by the UN Charter — "All Members shall refrain in their international relations from the threat or use of force against the territorial integrity or political independence of any state"[27] - had to be re-examined.

Pre-Emptive or Preventive Action?

"For centuries, international law recognized that nations need not suffer an attack before they can lawfully take action to defend themselves against forces that present an imminent danger of attack," acknowledged in 2002, *The National Security Strategy of the United States of America*, in an attempt to justify pre-emption. "Legal scholars and international jurists often conditioned the legitimacy of pre-emption on the existence of an imminent threat."[28]

However, the notion of pre-emptive war must be distinguished from the classical definition of preventive war — that which prevents another country or group of countries from *developing* the military potential to pose a serious threat. In other words, the "imminent danger of attack" has not yet materialized. The aim was to defuse long-term risk, not to defend against imminent attack. The document blurs these distinctions, first by using the terms "pre-emptive" and "preventive" interchangeably. More pointedly, it seeks to redefine the very concept of "imminent danger of attack" by somehow equating "the capabilities and objectives of today's adversaries" with their potential reliance on weapons of mass destruction. Regardless, Article 51 of the UN Charter is clear on the issue: the right of self-defense applies only "if an armed attack occurs."

The arguments invoked by the Bush administration to justify its military intervention in Iraq were quite similar to those employed by Israel in 1981, in the aftermath of its air strike against the Iraqi nuclear reactor at Osirak. The Israeli government argued that it had acted to prevent Iraq from developing nuclear weapons, a direct threat to Israel and, more broadly, to the stability of the entire region. For Israel, it was a matter of long-term national security. The Security Council saw the situation differently and unanimously passed a strongly worded resolution condemning "the military attack by Israel in clear violation with the Charter of the United Nations and the norms of international conduct."[29] Even the U.S. delegation voted in favor of this diplomatic tongue-lashing, but only because Israel, its staunch ally, had failed to "exhaust peaceful means for the resolution of this dispute."[30]

International scholars were nearly unanimous in their condemnation, with a few noteworthy exceptions. Anthony D'Amato, a professor at Northwestern School of Law, argued in support of Israel's action. In view of the "uniqueness of the nuclear weapons as a threat to systemic stability," Israel, he contended, "acted as a proxy for the international community."[31] Therefore, "for the stake [of] global survival," a preventive attack can be justified under certain conditions:

• "The pre-emptive strike has to be against a nuclear weapons facility and not against any other kind of weaponry;

• The target state must be a rogue state in the sense that it is unstable and is likely to use its nuclear weapons for international blackmail and aggrandizement;

- The pre- emptive strike must be limited to the nuclear facility target and must be carried out with the least possible loss of life; and

- The international community must be de facto disabled from carrying out the strike itself, thus implicitly authorizing an attack state to act as proxy for the international community."

D'Amato concluded the Security Council's condemnation was nothing short of hypocritical, for, in the end, "There was no mention of punishment in the resolution," making it at best "a gentle pat in the wrist." In the meanwhile, "the international community [...] was breathing a sigh of relief." Israel had done their dirty work.

In truth, D'Amato's arguments in support of Israel's strike against Iraq presented a narrow view of the problem. A broader analysis of recent preventive wars is more persuasive *against* the notion of preventive military action. For one thing, a preventive war remains contrary to international law and the principle of collective security as it has been established since 1919. "Norms, rules, standards of conduct, understandings about what is and is not permissible still count in international relations, now more than ever," wrote Paul W. Schroeder, professor emeritus at the University of Illinois, in 20002. "They form a central component of essential values in international politics."[32]

Secondly, the launching of a preventive military action against a potential enemy when there is no imminent threat creates a dangerous precedent, particularly when it is initiated by as powerful a state as the U.S. By applying the Bush Doctrine to past conflicts, one could rewrite and justify dubious wars. A good example is Austria's punitive military action against Serbia in the summer of 1914, which led to Germany's declarations of war against France and Russia a few days later. On August 3, in an address to the Reichstag, the German Chancellor, Theobald von Bethmann-Hollweg informed parliament that German troops were advancing on France after occupying Luxembourg and passing through Belgium: "Our invasion of Belgium is contrary to international law but the wrong — I speak openly — that we are committing we will make good as soon as our military goal has been reached."[33] The next day he also referred to the Treaty of London guaranteeing Belgian neutrality and signed by all the European powers including Prussia in 1839 as a "scrap of paper." The Bush administration and the German government of 1914 were equally willing to ignore international agreements in the name of military expediency.

Proponents of preventive military action tend to rely on contemporary history to bolster their case. The failure to act preventively, they argue, led to tragedies of monumental proportions. Winston Churchill wrote that Nazi Germany could have been stopped had Britain and France insisted on "[the] strict enforcement [...] of the disarmament clauses of the [Paris] Peace Treaty."[34] The Munich agreement of 1938 and British Prime Minister Chamberlain's overall policy of appeasement have repeatedly been used to illustrate the dire consequences of inaction against a determined potential enemy.

The problem is that analogies can be misleading, particularly if the example at hand is not put into context. In the case of the Munich agreement, Hitler boastfully exaggerated the scale of German rearmament, while engaging in highly successful tactics of bluff and threat, a policy known as "peaceful aggression." By 1938, Hitler was convinced he could achieve his ambitious expansionist goals without resorting to war, or at worst through localized conflicts. A general war was not foreseen.

The consequences of the Munich agreement proved disastrous for the Western democracies. The Franco-British capitulation marked a crucial psychological turning point in inter-war diplomacy. Great Britain and France lost their prestige and credibility, and the previously un-aligned Soviet Union was moved to reassess its priorities, entering negotiations with Nazi Germany. Thus, it may be argued that the outbreak of war in 1939 was a direct consequence of the Munich agreement in 1938. However, even with hindsight, it is impossible to determine whether a preventive military action would have been entirely successful at stopping Hitler. A preventive action may not be military or strategically sound.

Preventive Action as a Military Strategy: The Importance of Intelligence and Planning

Military strategists have engaged in lengthy debates over the overall success of a preventive action. According to Steven Prebeck, a former Major with the

U.S. Air Force, "preventive attacks are politically untenable and are not militarily possible."[35] History concurs, one glaring example being Japan's aggressive strategy toward the U.S. in 1941. In an attempt to curb Japanese expansionism, even at the risk of speeding up the march to war, the U.S. froze all Japanese assets in America, and forbade the export of commodities to Japan, thus denying the country 80 percent of its oil imports. The consequences were devastating. Without American oil, Japan could not sustain its war against China and pursue its main goal of a new order in Greater East Asia.

Japan maintained diplomatic negotiations with the U.S. but that was nothing more than a ploy to gain time for the military, which was planning its own preventive strike. The Japanese surprise attack against the U.S. Pacific fleet at Pearl Harbor was a success as far as it was. But ultimately the Japanese failed on two counts: the aircraft carriers were not at anchor and could not be destroyed; meanwhile, the naval dockyards and oil storage tanks were left intact. The U.S. forces regrouped and six months later they triumphed at the Battle of Midway. The only thing that Japan's preventive strike prevented was its own further expansion.

In the 1990s, as Washington pondered its response to North Korea's growing nuclear threat, Prebeck warned against preventive action. He argued that the U.S. lacked the military intelligence and technology required to destroy existing nuclear heads and "fixed manufacturing and production capabilities." Overall, a military action appeared risky, as North

Korea "could use the remaining warheads to retaliate against its neighbors," South Korea or Japan. A "sustained preventive attack" would have been needed, he concluded, with the disadvantage of making the United States the aggressor against a much less powerful nation. Prebeck appeared to have accurately assessed the limitations of American Intelligence.

The Bush administration faced similar accusations. It had portrayed a full-scale preventive action against Iraq as the only way to stop a rogue state "and [its] terrorist clients before they are able to threaten or use weapons of mass destruction." In February 2003, Secretary of State Colin Powell addressed a plenary session of the UN Security Council in New York City, making a case for military intervention in Iraq. "There can be no doubt that Saddam Hussein has biological weapons and the capability to rapidly produce more, many more,"[36] he declared. There was also "no doubt in [his] mind" that Iraq was actively developing a military nuclear program, an added threat to the already fragile Middle East. As it turned out, the alleged WMDs were never found, drawing accusations that the Bush administration had acted on faulty intelligence. "[The] analysis relied heavily on old information acquired largely before late 1998 and was strongly influenced by untested, long-held assumptions," concluded a report by the Kerr Group released in 2004. As a result, the findings "were seriously flawed, misleading and even wrong."[37] During an interview with Barbara Walters in 2005, when asked about his speech to the Security Council, Powell admitted the erroneous information he presented in 2003 would remain a "blot" on his records.

The administration's own record would be further blotted by the absence of an effective plan to manage the post-war period, beyond establishing a new democratic government. *The National Security Strategy of the USA* took great pains to reassure America's allies that Washington would "always proceed deliberately, weighing the consequences of our actions." That statement was in bald counterpoint to reality. Such lack of foresight beyond initial "victory" underscores the danger of preventive wars. Unless all options are carefully reviewed and debated, a myopic strategy can produce unintended and controversial results.

In the complex case of Iraq, the Bush administration clearly gave insufficient consideration to the country's colonial past. In 1920, Iraq was created artificially by the United Kingdom, chopped from the dismembered corpse of the old Ottoman Empire. The country's borders strained against the turmoil of ethnic and religious divisions: three very distinct communities — the Kurds in the north, the Sunnis in the centre and the Shiites in the south — were ill-prepared to live together. Well before Iraq's first anniversary, the Shiites revolted against their British occupiers, a surprise attack that claimed 2,200 casualties and, by one account, more money than it had taken to finance the Arab overthrow of the Ottomans.

This should have constituted a valuable lesson for the Americans eight decades later. But, by all evidence, it went unheeded. The American intervention in Iraq destroyed a precarious political and religious balance of power and spread the risks of civil war between the majority Shiites and the Sunni minority that governed under Saddam Hussein.

Furthermore, America's preventive war divided the region into two opposing fronts: the consenting states (Kuwait and Saudi Arabia) and those hostile to the American presence (Syria and Iran). The war has also stymied the ever-difficult peace process between Israel and the Palestinians. The future for Iraq and the entire region remains very uncertain. In 2008, even the U.S. Department of Defense had to admit that, even though "the security, political and economic trends in Iraq continue to be positive, they remain fragile, reversible and uneven."[38]

Above all, the War on Terror has taken a turn for the worst precisely because American intervention has greatly contributed to the development of radical Islamist movements in Iraq, contrary to the stated objectives of the Bush administration.

The Political and Diplomatic Consequences of a Preventive Strategy

The American intervention in Iraq has had serious political and diplomatic implications. American prestige in the world has declined sharply since 2001. The U.S. is now widely regarded as a bully, threatening those that oppose its will, or even simply disagree. George W. Bush's unilateral foreign policy approach has alienated many countries, including traditional allies such as Canada. Governments did not appreciate being lectured by a nation that repeatedly rejected a world system based on collective security and the notion that global issues can be resolved through negotiation and compromise. In 2002 a European Foreign Minister was said to have declared: "we have never seen such disdain from Washington. Not only is there a complete absence of consultation, but there is an exaltation of unilateralism and the militarization of foreign policy thinking."[39]

This growing resentment has already damaged American influence in the world. The preventive action against Iraq, in the face of global opposition, only worsened Washington's image. When a superpower targets a much lesser power, whatever the reasons may be, the populations are bound to see themselves as the victims of a ruthless aggressor, thus offering their support tacitly or explicitly to terrorist organizations. For neighboring nations — Iran is a good example — the anger and frustration can lead to a siege mentality. The Iranians need only map out the U.S. presence in the Middle East to feel encircled. Iranians also remember that their country was partially occupied by the Soviet Union in 1941; their government collapsed in 1953 thanks to the intervention of the CIA; American commandos penetrated their territory in 1979 during the hostage crisis, and their country was attacked by Iraq in September 1980. For Iran, the development of nuclear programs has become a question of national security. By favoring a preventive military action against Iraq, it is likely the Bush administration helped reinforce Tehran's perceptions of encirclement and peril.

The geopolitical consequences of a military preventive action must not be underestimated. When

Washington acted without UN approval, turning a deaf ear to close traditional allies that had reservations about Iraq, it greatly diminished the credibility of the United Nations; more importantly perhaps, the Bush administration's blatant unilateralism and seeming arrogance put a strain on some old alliances. The decision to encourage "a coalition of the willing" against Iraq divided NATO and the European Union – the same body that had pledged all help and support in the wake of the 9/11 attacks. No one then had denied Washington the right to strike at terrorists. "The European Council is totally supportive of the American people in the face of the deadly terrorist attacks. On the basis of Security Council Resolution 1368, a riposte by the U.S. is legitimate," a joint statement said. Just two years later, the common front was a faded memory. In a resounding speech to the United Nations Security Council in March 2003, Dominique de Villepin, the French Foreign Minister, warned that "the choice is […] between two visions of the world. To those who choose to use force and think they can resolved the world's complex problems through swift and preventive action, we argue the need for determined action over time."[40]

Two months earlier, eight European leaders had released a joint statement calling for "firm international cohesion" in the struggle "against terrorism and the proliferation of weapons of mass destruction," and supporting the United States in its decision "to get rid the world of the danger posed by Saddam Hussein's" regime.[41] The European Union was no longer unified.

As Neta Crawford, a professor of political science at Boston University pointed out, "whether states and groups armed because they were afraid or because they have aggressive intentions, instability is likely to grow as a preventive war doctrine creates the mutual fear of surprise attack."[42] By launching a large-scale preventive war against Iraq, the United States opened a Pandora's Box. In a world of geopolitical hotspots and international tensions, preventive military action is an unnecessarily destabilizing force, and also a bad example. What if other nations were to follow suit in the belief that preventive action can protect from perceived threats

Chapter 2

Canada and the War on Terror "Made in USA": Border Security and Immigration

From 2001 on, and for as long as George W. Bush remained in office, America's traditional allies were faced with a choice: embrace his administration's crusade for democracy and near-obsession with security, or oppose them, even if only by default. "Either you are with us or you are with the terrorists," declared the president a few days after the 9/11 attacks. In Washington, it was expected Canada would naturally be "with us."

At first, the relationship appeared as strong as ever. "I was stricken by news and television pictures coming from the United States this morning," said Canadian Prime Minister Jean Chrétien, in a statement issued on September 11, 2001. "It is impossible to fully comprehend the evil that would have conjured up such a cowardly and depraved assault upon thousands of innocent people. We stand ready to provide any assistance that our American friends may need at this very, very difficult hour and in the subsequent investigation."[43] On that fateful day, Canadians of all stripes were united in shock and disbelief with their American neighbors. With North American airspace swiftly shut down, communities across Canada spontaneously offered refuge to thousands of stranded air travellers.

Soon, however, the outpouring of grief and support was replaced by doubt and acrimony on both sides. The U.S. government's investigation quickly focused on Osama bin Laden and al-Qaeda, and officials in Washington wasted no time in pointing fingers at alleged lax Canadian security. They believed some of the hijackers were likely to have entered the United States from Canada. The accusations would prove to be groundless. Nevertheless, they helped cement Canada's image in the minds of official Washington: "soft on terrorism" and a haven for terrorists. The reputation has lingered ever since.

Canadians got an early sign of Washington's displeasure when President Bush, during his September 20 address to a joint session of Congress, failed to include Canada in the list of 15 allies and friends he praised for their support. Canada's loyalties came into further question two years later when its Liberal government declined to join Bush's "Coalition of the Willing" in the invasion of Iraq.

By the time Bush was re-elected in 2004, the War on Terror had cost the U.S. much of the international sympathy that had naturally accrued after the 9/11 attacks. Many political pundits and a majority of the American public openly criticized the president's positions and the Iraq quagmire. Bush's successor, President Barack Obama, has pledged his administration will dramatically alter course, but it will take some time to rescue America's image in the world.

After all, the Bush administration spent seven years reshaping the U.S. government to reflect its ideas on the new nature of war. The country that likes to portray itself as a beacon of democracy chose to dismiss or reinterpret international law conventions, deeming them "obstacles" in the global fight against terrorist activities.

As far as respect for human rights is concerned, 9/11 marked a turning point for the U.S. It pushed aside international law to reintroduce torture and prison abuse at its infamous prison at Guantanamo Bay, Cuba. The U.S. detained suspected terrorists without evidence, including a Canadian citizen, Maher Arar. In 2002, the young wireless-technology consultant was interrogated at Kennedy Airport in New York and then flown to his native Syria, where he was deprived of international jurisprudence. Canadians were greatly alarmed by the case of Maher Arar and, more generally, by the "Fortress America" mentality that increasingly marked U.S. decisions on national security. Was Canada's special relationship with the U.S. being eroded by paranoia and reactionism? What could be done to preserve Canadian interests?

"Fortress America": The USA PATRIOT Act, Homeland Security and Other Tales

Having declared war on international terrorism in the days following the 9/11 attacks, the Bush administration quickly developed an ambitious and controversial series of policies at home and abroad, policies that inevitably affected Canada. On September 18, 2001, Congress authorized the use of force against the Taliban in Afghanistan, and soon thereafter a US-led coalition launched Operation Enduring Freedom. But military action was only the tip of the iceberg. As President Bush and his close advisors were prompt to acknowledge, the struggle to defeat terrorism could only turn into a long, protracted war against a transnational, highly organized and ideologically motivated threat. "Our enemies are in a unique position, and they are a unique brand of ideological extremists whose vision of the world is best summed up by how the Taliban ran Afghanistan," testified the Commander of the United States Central Command, General John Abizaid, in 2004. "Our enemies kill without remorse, they challenge our will through the careful manipulation of propaganda and information, they seek safe havens in order to develop weapons of mass destruction [...]" The nature of the "enemies" being so different and potentially lethal, the War on Terror so "unconventional," the United States and its allies cannot "win this thing militarily alone."[44]

General Abizaid was only the latest high-ranking military official to publicly embrace the White House' strategy against global terrorism as proposed after the September 11 attacks, that is a "continuous action against terrorist groups, the cumulative effect of which will initially disrupt, over time degrade, and ultimately destroy the terrorist organizations"[45] through military and non-military activities. On September 14, 2001, when George W. Bush declared a state of national emergency "by reasons of certain terrorist attacks,"[46] his administration was ready to push for a brand new array of anti- and counter-terrorism measures. It translated into a national strategy for Homeland Security to prevent "terrorist attacks within the United States," and a national strategy for combating terrorism aimed at "identifying and diffusing threats before they reach our borders." In a matter of weeks, eradicating global terrorism became the central element of Washington's national security policy. The price security proved costly: the trampling on individual freedoms and liberties as a young Canadian of Syrian descent, Maher Arar, was soon to discover.

A mere six weeks after the 9/11 tragedy, as the U.S. was still reeling from two waves of deadly anthrax attacks, a paralyzed Congress bowed to the Bush administration's repeated pressures and overwhelmingly adopted the USA PATRIOT Act, hastily drafted and, at 342 pages, rather cumbersome. None of the proposed amendments (to water down the act) was passed, and the Act was promptly signed into law by President Bush. The White House now had new and far-reaching law enforcement powers in many key areas, including surveillance procedures, the protection of borders, immigration and international money laundering.

Section 802 created a brand new federal crime known as "domestic terrorism" that extended the definition of terrorism to include "acts dangerous to human life that are a violation of the criminal laws [if they] appear to be intended [...] to influence the policy of a government by intimidation or coercion," and if they "occur primarily within the territorial jurisdiction of the United States." The wording was left purposely vague to allow federal law enforcement agencies flexibility in their interpretation of the new concept. Thus, anti-war activists or organizations could be seen as intending to influence government policy through coercion, and acts of civil disobedience could easily be construed as "acts dangerous to human life." The most controversial measures allowed for the greater use of surveillance and control mechanisms, obviously against American citizens but also, and perhaps more importantly, against non-Americans or "aliens." Section 412 of the Act is particularly discriminatory against "aliens," authorizing the Attorney General to "maintain into custody" for a period of seven days and "for additional periods of up to six months," without the possible intervention of a judge, any alleged "terrorist aliens" until they are "removed from the United States."

The USA PATRIOT Act was initially portrayed as temporary legislation that would expire at the end of 2005. But in July 2005, both houses of Congress passed the first of two reauthorization bills, the USA Patriot and Terrorism Prevention Reauthorization Act of 2005. "The Patriot Act has accomplished exactly what it was designed to do," boasted George W. Bush, the following year, when he signed the second bill, the USA PATRIOT Improvement and Reauthorization Act. "It has helped us detect terror cells, disrupt terrorist plots and save American lives. The bill I sign today extends these vital provisions. It also gives our nation new protections and added defenses [...] while we safeguard the civil liberties of our people."[47] President Bush may have believed his own reassuring words with regard to civil liberties, but to this day the USA Patriot

Act of 2001 and the subsequent reauthorization bills stand out as dramatic ruptures in American democracy. It can be argued that what began as a temporary and exceptional measure born out of urgency has become a permanent legal fixture that sacrifices basic freedoms in the name of the War on Terror.

Canada, A "Haven" for Terrorists?

Canadians generally viewed the USA PATRIOT Act and the creation of a Department of Homeland Security as yet more evidence of America's growing paranoia in the face of danger. Some provincial governments acted quickly to prevent U.S. Law enforcement agencies from obtaining personal data about Canadian citizens without their knowledge or consent, a move that was derided as doing more harm than good. More troubling, perhaps, were the allegations that some of the hijackers had likely entered the United States from Canada.[48] Reaction in Canada ranged from disbelief to outright outrage. Elinor Caplan, the federal immigration minister at the time, flatly denied that Canada was harbouring any terrorists at all. As it turned out, all 19 hijackers were trained in the U.S. (For all its deficiencies, the Canadian immigration system never made a blunder as embarrassing as its American counterparts: the U.S. Immigration Service processed the visas of some 9/11 terrorists *after* the attacks had taken place.) However, Canadians ought not to have been surprised at American willingness to point fingers northward.

Canada's reputation for being soft on terrorism was by then firmly established on both sides of the border.

At the time of the 9/11 attacks, Canada was no stranger to terrorism. In June 1985, Sikh terrorists allegedly downed an Air India flight on its way from Canada to London, killing all 329 passengers and crew on board. After the initial flurry of media scrutiny, however, talk of terrorism quickly receded. In 1997, following the deadly attack on a U.S. military facility in Saudi Arabia, one of the suspects was traced to Canada. The FBI requested Canada's help to put the man under surveillance leading up to his arrest, only to be told that no funding nor appropriate staff was available to conduct such an operation. Two years later, Algerian refugee claimant Ahmed Ressam, carrying a fake Canadian passport, was arrested as he tried to enter the U.S. with a car full of explosives. He had intended to drive to Los Angeles and blow up the airport. "How the Canadians had missed the cell [Ressam belonged to in Montreal] was difficult to understand,"[49] observed Richard Clarke, Clinton and Bush's former National Coordinator for Security Infrastructure Protection and Counterterrorism.

It was, therefore, unsurprising that Americans would regard Canada with suspicion in the aftermath of the 9/11 attacks. During the brief debate on the passage of the USA PATRIOT Act, Senator Byron Dorgan of North Dakota noted that many ports of entry at the U.S.-Canada border were left unguarded at night, with the only sentry being "an orange rubber cone, just a big old orange rubber cone… [I]t cannot talk, it cannot walk. It cannot shoot. It cannot tell a terrorist from a tow truck. It is just a big fat dumb rubber cone sitting in the middle the road [...] That is supposed to be security in this country."[50] In April 2002, the CBS newsmagazine *60 Minutes* aired a segment titled "al-Qaeda in Canada," a damaging piece that depicted without nuance or understanding Canada's "ultra liberal" immigration system. It criticized the country's social welfare system as too generous and, therefore, bound to attract criminals and terrorists.

Critics in Canada have echoed the stinging statements of Senator Dorgan and *60 Minutes*. In 2004, Canadian journalist Stewart Bell claimed Canada had become the safest refuge in the world for international terrorism, "a country with an unguarded open back door, where extremists are tolerated and free to conspire and act," primarily because of lax immigration, refugee and tax policies. As an example, he pointed at the activities of the Liberation Tigers of Tamil Eelam (LTTE), more commonly known as the Tamil Tigers, an organization identified as "terrorist" by more than thirty countries. For years, the Canadian government failed to take any action against the LTTE and its dubious fundraising campaigns, until the Conservative government, elected in 2006, announced it was banning the organization altogether.

Bell insisted that Canadian law enforcement agencies were not the problem. In fact, "they have been effective at monitoring the activities of terrorist groups operating in Canada, but they have been unable to put them out of business, in large part because their political masters have not given them the tools they need to do so."[51]

Bell's was hardly a lone voice. A flurry of books appeared in the wake of 9/11, lamenting Canada's weak immigration policies and the government's failure to bolster them.[52] But beyond Conservative and big business circles, they were not all that well received by a Canadian public more interested in health care and economic issues than immigration and security. "Terrorism is seen as a fairly modest, even minor, component of a much broader and more multidimensional security hierarchy in Canada," revealed a comparative study by Canadian polling firm EKOS Research Associates and the American Enterprise Institute in 2005. "Indeed, for nearly half of Canadians, the 'War on Terror' is an apocryphal exaggeration, whereas this remains a key national project in the United States. Despite the more tepid concern about terrorism in Canada, support for security measures remains stalwart."[53]

Call it naïveté — scholar and current opposition leader Michael Ignatieff labeled it "naïve narcissism" — or just wishful thinking, a majority of Canadians continue to believe, notwithstanding ominous warnings, that their country is less exposed to terrorism than is the U.S. In truth, Canada is as exposed as any democratic, secular and liberal Western society. "We stand for everything that al-Qaeda doesn't like,"[54] Ignatieff noted. In November 2002, Osama bin Laden allegedly issued one of his statements, threatening countries that supported the American War on Terror. Canadian Security Intelligence Service (CSIS) promptly warned that "while there is currently no specific threat to Canada, Canada is not insulated from terrorism and [...] threats can escalate against all of us allied in the struggle against terrorism."⁵⁵ Canada's mission in Afghanistan, albeit greatly controversial at home, is an important factor in assessing the likelihood of a terrorist attack on Canadian soil. As long as Canadian troops fight in that country, Canada will automatically remain on the list of potential targets. Finally, Canada's close economic ties with the U.S. make some key shared infrastructures vulnerable to threats. It should come as no surprise that American officials immediately pointed fingers at Canada when the North American electrical grid collapsed in the summer of 2003, plunging millions of citizens into darkness. The Severe Acute Respiratory Syndrome (SARS) crisis, also in 2003, cast further doubt on Canada's readiness to prevent and contain biological or chemical attacks.

Immigration has long been the main engine of population growth in Canada and, more than that, it has become a core component of Canadian identity. A powerful national myth holds that immigration has shaped Canada into a gentle, peace-loving and, above all, multicultural society, a mosaic of various ethnic groups willing to live together in peace.

However, new arrivals increasingly are coming from Asia and the Middle East as opposed to Europe. Inevitably, some new immigrants in recent years have left war torn regions and may still be sympathizing with one faction or another. As the CSIS reported in May 2000: "Most immigrants or refugees coming to Canada do so only to seek a peaceful existence, often fleeing violent conflicts. In some cases, however, these conflicts are difficult to leave behind." The agency warned that preventing the spread of foreign-born conflicts into Canada requires constant monitoring of organizations with possible links to international terrorism. "The support activities of terrorist groups here are far more prevalent [than in the U.S.],"[56] warned the report.

Another document made public in June 2001 predicted that "a hardening attitude and a willingness on the part of certain terrorist organizations to directly support terrorist operations in North America reinforce the belief that Canadians, now more than ever, are potential victims and Canada a potential venue for terrorist attacks."[57] Neither report received much attention upon their release. Clearly, security issues did not rank very high among the government's priorities.

Washington's perception of Canada as unprepared and "soft on terrorism", whether fair or not, would only further weaken a "special relationship" already strained since 2001.

The Case of Maher Arar

The September 11 attacks may have forced Canadians to re-examine their relationship with the United States, but according to polling, they "are no more likely to want to be U.S. citizens or feel that [they] have become any more American in recent years."[58] Since 2001, Canadians have been more eager than ever to cultivate their difference, which explains their great reluctance at contemplating too deep a reform of the existing immigration system. Such reform would necessarily go against Canadian traditions of openness and tolerance. Yet, reform is needed. As Arne Kislenko, a professor of contemporary history at Ryerson University clearly demonstrated, "There are myriad problems at Canada's borders, most undetected or ill-considered by the Canadian public. Some are systemic and stem from immigration legislation and regulations. Others [...] resolve around procedure, training, and other dynamics of bureaucracy."[59]

There is no doubt Canada's immigration and refugee system needs improvement, just as U.S. critics have alleged. However, some measures have already been taken. In 2001, the Canadian Parliament voted a new Refugee and Immigration Protection Act, a "clearer, modern legislation to ensure that Canada's immigration and refugee protection system is able to respond to new challenges and opportunities." The new legislation's main purpose was to prevent potential criminals and terrorists from settling in Canada; it's many provisions included better cooperation between provinces and foreign states, tightened inadmissibility provisions, and clear detention criteria.[60]

In December 2004, after months of negotiation, Canada and the U.S. implemented the Safe Third Country Agreement. It requires that refugee claimants make their claim in the first of the two countries they arrive in, the idea being that either country is deemed safe for refugees. Officially, the purpose of the agreement was to better manage "the flow of refugee claimants at the shared land border."[61] But, as critics have argued, it is flawed on three counts. First, it is much easier for far-flung refugees to find a direct flight to the U.S., which means claimants heading for Canada are more likely to travel via a U.S. airport.

Second, it is a known fact that U.S. Customs and Immigration, under the USA Patriot Act, have not shied from using detention as a means to deter claimants from seeking asylum in North America. In 2007, in a stunning decision, Justice Michael Phelan of the Federal Court of Canada ruled that the Safe Third Country Agreement violated refugee rights and that the U.S. did not meet the conditions to be considered a safe country. Furthermore, Justice Phelan stated that "the U.S. does not meet the Refugee Convention requirements nor the Convention against Torture prohibition,"[62] a statement that greatly embarrassed the Canadian government, which immediately launched an appeal.

Although never mentioned in the final statement, the case of Maher Arar must have been a factor in Justice Phelan's consideration, an affair that caused outrage in Canada and put a permanent stain on the Canada-U.S. security relationship. Arar, a Canadian citizen of Syrian background, was a frequent business traveler to the U.S. when he was stopped, detained and interrogated at New York's Kennedy airport in September 2002. He was transferred to a detention facility where he remained in solitary confinement for a period of two weeks, without access to a lawyer. Arar was suspected of being an al-Qaeda operative in Canada and, for reasons of national security, was eventually deported to his native Syria, where he was allegedly beaten and tortured. Critics have long argued it was never a case of deportation, for the U.S.

government would then have sent Arar back to Canada for further investigation, but a blatant example of rendition, or torture by proxy. Proponents of rendition may regard the practice as legally and politically acceptable in the case of terror leaders. The point here is that U.S. authorities were acting on suspicions alone yet they deported Arar to Syria, a country known for torturing detainees.[63] At that time, Syria was actively working with the U.S. on the terror front, as was acknowledged by the State Department and the CIA.[64]

Facing public outcry, the new Canadian Prime Minister, Paul Martin, discussed the matter of Arar's deportation with George W. Bush in 2004. The U.S. government subsequently agreed to keep Ottawa informed should a Canadian citizen be arrested, detained and deported on suspicion of terrorist activities. Canadian human rights experts criticized the agreement as "ineffective and legally unenforceable."[65]

In 2006, Martin's successor, Prime Minister Stephen Harper, called on the U.S. government "to come clean" on the Maher Arar affair and sought Washington's assurances that "these kind of incidents will not be repeated in the future."[66] The U.S. government responded evasively and, to date, Arar's name has yet to be removed from Washington's terrorist watch list.

The Canadian government's reaction to the case brings to light the many difficulties in balancing international security with basic freedoms in the post 9/11 era, particularly for a country that is fundamentally attached to its traditions of openness, diversity and tolerance. The debate about North American security is ongoing, and there is no indication it will stop anytime soon. Some people, usually on the right of the political spectrum, have called for even greater cooperation with Washington, advocating for "a North American community of law."[67]

But for all its many flaws, Canada's immigration system has shaped our country for decades. While it needs to be updated, it all needs to be preserved, But, there is not the slightest evidence the whole system has made Canada or North America less secure. The Federal Court's ruling of 2007 — the one that deemed the U.S. unsafe for refugee claimants — only served to emphasize the importance of remaining vigilant in the face of Washington's zealous approach to security and immigration. Great hopes have grown around the election of Barack Obama and his promise of change. The new president's decision to close the prison at Guantanamo Bay is indeed a hopeful sign. But the pressure from Washington is likely to continue as national security remains a central U.S. preoccupation in the years to come.

Sharing a Continent

The story of Maher Arar is only the best-known example in Canada of Washington's aggressive response to the 9/11 attacks. They represent a worrying trend for the many Canadians who oppose cultural and regulatory assimilation by the U.S., for fear of losing their identity and sovereignty. However, proponents of further continental integration warn that preserving the status quo or doing too little may come at a price, especially because our two economies are now so highly interdependent. They have a point. Despite tendencies among the three NAFTA members to revert to protectionism in some instances, economic integration has dramatically increased in the past two decades. In recent years, nearly 85 percent of all Canadian exports were shipped either to or through the U.S., the highest percentage of any industrialized countries. Similarly, Canada is the main trading partner of some thirty-nine American states. Those economic ties were acknowledged by Hillary Clinton at the time of her confirmation hearings for Secretary of State. "In our efforts to return to economic growth here in the United States, we have an especially critical need to work more closely with Canada, our largest trading partner and Mexico, our third largest," she declared. "Canada and Mexico are also our biggest suppliers of imported energy."[68]

Those were reassuring words for Canada; however, the inescapable reality is that the U.S. far outweighs its two partners in every domain. Canada's overwhelming dependence on the American economy cannot be underestimated, particularly given the post-9/11 context and Washington's quasi-obsession with security.

The attacks on September 11, 2001 were a defining moment for all of us, a moment we will never forget. That morning, I happened to be on my way back to Toronto from Paris where I had attended my brother's wedding a few days prior. The first sign of trouble came when the captain announced that, "because of problems in the United States," we would be landing in Montreal instead of Toronto. The severity of the situation was kept from us until we landed. By the time we left the aircraft, it had become clear something terrible had happened. People stood clustered in front of TV screens in the terminal to see footage of the planes smashing into the World Trade Center, the scenes of panic in the streets of New York and eventually the Twin Towers coming down. In the days that followed, like so many of my fellow Canadians, I felt very much a part of the mass sympathy for the American people. On September 14, I walked to the American consulate in Toronto, where people were gathering as part of a national day of mourning. At the government level, Prime Minister Jean Chrétien purposely avoided the limelight — eager to show proper support for the U.S. without appearing to embrace the enflamed rhetoric that came from Washington.

Chrétien's reaction was very much in tune with his propensity to maintain a "good — and not too cozy" relationship with the U.S. The moment he became Prime Minister, in 1993, he made it clear Canadian foreign policy would not necessarily walk in tandem with Washington's. It was a sharp departure from his predecessor, Brian Mulroney, who took great pains to foster warm relations with his American counterpart. Chrétien was able to keep his distance with little criticism as long as Bill Clinton was in office. But everything changed with the arrival of George W. Bush. The new president's Texan roots naturally endowed him with a perspective that had little room for Canada: he looked southward instead of north, and his conservative political background made him suspicious of Canada's relatively "liberal" policies. It also irked the U.S. administration that Canada's military was in a dire state of neglect, thanks to years of budget-cutting under Liberal rule. Many in the Pentagon and at the White House considered Canada a weak partner in continental security. The relationship was already seriously strained when the attacks on September 11, 2001 took place.

At first, it looked like Canada-U.S. relations would largely weather that fateful day. After all, Canada had played its part, welcoming some two hundred flights diverted from American airspace. The Prime Minister was very happy to announce that President Bush "called me many times and he was always extremely grateful for what Canada has done." The illusion of normalcy would soon fade. On September 20, Bush made an impassioned speech to a joint session of Congress, in which he outlined his War on Terror and thanked some fifteen countries that had already joined him in this new endeavour. But he did not thank Canada. The Chrétien government played down the omission, arguing it was of no consequence and that Canadians should not read too much into it. The next day, U.S. Secretary of State Colin Powell was quick to publicly thank Canada for being "the first on the scene with all kinds of help for us in this time of crisis, […] a sign of the close relationship that exists between our two countries and our two peoples."[69] The Canadian public and the media took it more personally.

"Canada gets Bush-whacked,"[70] yelled the bold tabloid headline of the *Toronto Sun* on September 21. Another daily, the *National Post*, argued the presidential snub was a sure reflection of White House concerns over Canada's diminished military resources and lacklustre counterterrorism performance.[71]

With respect to trade, foreign policy and, of course, security, the implications of Washington's perceived coldness were also obvious. Trade was perhaps the biggest issue, as any lasting disruption would have grave consequences for the Canadian economy. In the aftermath of 9/11, the U.S. imposed drastic new processes for border screening, slowing to a trickle, at least temporarily, the critical cross-border movement of goods and people. Business leaders in Canada reeled as they assessed their mounting financial losses. Something had to be done, and quickly. The government of Canada acted decisively to prevent cross-border trade — worth some $500 billion annually — from collapsing altogether. Negotiations at the highest levels took place in late 2001, leading to a joint declaration and a 30-point action plan. The main purpose was to develop a "Smart Border" arrangement between the two countries to facilitate the movement of low-risk shipments and travellers, using new technologies and improving coordination between a number of Canadian and U.S. agencies. "The security of our two countries will be strengthened by the action plan,"[72] declared Canada's deputy Prime Minister at the press conference.

The success of the initiative prompted further dialogue, this time including Mexico. In March 2005,

George W. Bush, Mexican President Vincente Fox and then Canadian Prime Minister Paul Martin, announced a "Security and Prosperity Partnership," to provide better cooperation on security and economic issues within North America.[73]

Both the "Smart Border" and the "Security and Prosperity Partnership" initiatives were encouraging. They demonstrated it was possible to negotiate a viable compromise that balanced security measures with economic imperatives. Such a compromise was far more difficult when the U.S. decided to invade Iraq in 2003, for it forced Canada to review its role in North American security and contemplate sending troops in Afghanistan. They are still in operation today and are not scheduled to leave until February 2011.

Chapter 3

Canada's Contribution to the War on Terror 2001-2003: Canada, America's Best Friend?

The service and sacrifice of Canadian troops in the highly dangerous Kandahar region of Afghanistan remains the most tangible example of Canada's commitment to the global war against terrorism. Yet War on Terror is not a phrase that you will find in Canadian policy documents or tumbling from the lips of politicians, even when addressing the troops. "Your work is about more than just defending Canada's national interests," Prime Minister Stephen Harper told the troops in 2006. "Your work is also about demonstrating an international leadership role for our country."[74] That may have been a subtle way of saying that Canada was pulling its weight in the fight against terrorism. But, euphemisms aside, Canada's "leadership" came at a heavy cost in the form of new security practices and institutions.

As the northern neighbor and number one trading partner of the U.S., Canada could hardly have shied away from that country's War on Terror. We have seen that, pre-9/11, Washington already considered Canada an unreliable junior partner in rooting out terrorists and deflecting attacks. Post-9/11, the challenge was to provide sufficient support to the Americans without seeming to mimic their more contentious foreign and domestic policies.

Following the attacks against the World Trade Center and the Pentagon, the Liberals swiftly passed Bill C-36, also known as the Canadian Anti-Terrorism Act. They also negotiated a border security deal with the United States and gathered whatever troops and equipment they could find to mount an expeditionary force to Afghanistan.

While the USA Patriot Act was passed by wide margins in both houses of Congress, Bill C-36 was hotly debated in the Canadian House of Commons. Some proposed measures were denounced as infringements on civil liberties, a seeming capitulation to American interests. But was that really the case? Perhaps more significant was the decision to depart from the U.S. example and limit the definition of "terrorist activity" so that it fell in line with article 2 (1) (b) of the *International Convention for the Suppression of Financing of Terrorism* adopted by the United Nations in 1999. And in February 2007, when Bill C-36 was up for renewal, all three opposition parties rose as one to defeat two of its most controversial measures: one that empowered the authorities to detain suspects for three days without charge and another that permitted forced testimony before a judge.

The debate pitting national security against civil liberties will rage on for some time in Canada due to several factors. The current Conservative government favors tougher ongoing anti-terrorism legislation, but its minority position in Parliament means it can't act without some opposition support. Second, no Canadian government since 2001 has ever clearly determined where Canada's stand on the War on Terror actually is.

But could Canada continue to walk this tightrope on the War on Terror while gaining domestic support for national security matters? Apparently not. In early 2003, Canada abstained from backing the United States' unilateral decision to invade Iraq, casting much doubt, certainly in Washington, on Canada's commitment to the global war against terrorism.

Security: The New Priority

The attacks on the U.S. on September 11, 2001 propelled terrorism and security-related issues to the top of Canada's political agenda. The shift proved all the more dramatic because, for the first time, the government could measure the impact of terrorism on the economy. The closing of the Canada-U.S. border, in the days following the attacks, made it urgent to consider a re-alignment in all security matters, even just to show Washington that Canada was prepared to act decisively.

Jean Chrétien, the Prime Minister in office, issued a resolutely sympathetic statement of solidarity on the day of the attacks but otherwise remained on the sidelines. He declared September 14 a national day of mourning and attended a memorial service in Ottawa, but that was as far as he was willing to go. Thus he left much doubt as to what course Canada intended to follow with respect to the newly proclaimed War on Terror. Critics have long derided Chrétien "lackluster performance." Where was Mr. Chrétien when world leaders — British Prime Minister Tony Blair being the most eager of them all — were rushing to Washington to express the full support of their countries in those challenging times? "In a moment when statesmanship and decisiveness were required, our key political leaders were found wanting,"[75] writes for instance Jennifer Welsh, a Canadian professor who teaches international relations at Oxford.

Then, as the Bush administration made it clear that combating and eradicating international terrorism had just become the number one priority of U.S. national security policy, Chrétien hinted publicly that Canada would neither be turned "into a fortress against the world" nor would it be forced "to sacrifice [its] values or traditions under the pressure of urgent circumstances." Those were bold statements, attuned with the Prime Minister's long-time policy of supporting the American friend and ally but without necessarily agreeing on everything. Differences between the two countries had to be respected, and Chrétien would not be pressured by Washington on major issues, including continental security. "We like each other," the Prime Minister had declared shortly after his election in 1993. "I just don't want Canada to be perceived as the 51st state of America."[76] Given the magnitude of what had just happened in New York

City and Washington, D.C., it was perhaps the wrong time to reaffirm Canada's political distance, but it gave reassurance to many Canadians.

Behind the scenes, however, Canada's leadership was reacting with great speed to the 9/11 attacks. It was one thing to declare publicly Canada's "differences." But the inescapable reality was that continental relations had just dramatically shifted, and there was little time to waste. "Canada had to react not only to 9/11 but also to the American reaction to 9/11,"[77] wrote Canadian scholar Reg Whitaker. Two days after the attacks, the Prime Minister established an informal ad hoc committee to manage the immediate aftermath of the crisis and, on October 2, created another ad hoc committee on Public Security and Anti-terrorism, to be chaired by the Deputy Prime Minister, John Manley. These were strong indications that, political posturing aside, Canada was taking security issues very seriously. This second committee spearheaded the creation of Bill C-36, anti-terrorism legislation that was brought before Parliament in December.

Bill C-36 introduced sweeping changes to the Criminal Code of Canada for the purpose of "disabling and dismantling the activities of terrorists groups and those who support them." It made it a crime to collect or provide funds for the perpetration of terrorist activities, to facilitate such activities, to instruct "any person to carry out any activity for the benefit of [...] a terrorist group," and, finally, to harbor or conceal a terrorist.[78]

The bill also sanctioned the use of far-reaching new powers and tools for police forces, the national Royal Canadian Mounted Police (RCMP) and CSIS. They could now make preventive arrests and use electronic surveillance in a wider range of instances. Unlike the USA Patriot Act, which few U.S. politicians dared challenge, Canada's new legislation generated heated debates in the House of Commons over the curtailment of civil liberties.

Two clauses proved particularly controversial. One allowed the police to arrest alleged terrorists without a warrant and detain them for a period up to three days without charge, "to prevent the carrying out of terrorist activit[ies]." The other clause allowed a judge to consider whether it was appropriate to compel a detainee to testify in secret about pending terrorist acts or past associations and "commit the person to prison for a term not exceeding twelve months," should he or she refuse.

The Liberal majority rejected the opposition's proposed amendments and passed a motion to cut off debate. As a gesture of good will, however, the government added a "five-year sunset clause." The most controversial provisions would automatically expire in five years unless reinstated by parliament.

Meanwhile, Ottawa was preparing to table its annual budget, and national security was high on the agenda, despite the opposition of some cabinet ministers who rejected the imperative of enhanced bilateral security cooperation with the U.S. "Freedom to manoeuvre and to maintain some independence is really getting into some red zones,"[79] warned Lloyd Axworthy, Minister of Foreign Affairs. However, such dissenting views were overruled, and the legislation passed.

The splurge of security spending was unprecedented in Canadian history. $7.7 billion CAD of new funding was allocated over a period of five years to finance a series of national security related measures and the agencies that were to carry them out. Targeted programs included air security, intelligence (with a particular emphasis on improved cooperation between Canada's national security agencies), border security, critical infrastructure protection and emergency preparedness.

But the budget would be of no significant benefit to the Canadian military. Ottawa was anxious to align its security policy with the U.S., but at least at that stage, the possibility of full-scale military deployments was not on the table. Only those sections of the armed forces involved in anti- and counterterrorism activities, like the Canadian special operations force known as Joint Task Force 2, were to receive some much needed cash. The result was disappointing for the pro-military lobby in Ottawa, particularly since the question of a deployment had surfaced in the immediate aftermath of 9/11. On September 17, Stockwell Day, then leader of the Official Opposition had asked Prime Minister Chrétien whether he could "assure the House today that if the United States correctly identifies the sponsors of terrorism and engages in armed conflict, Canada will stand with the United States and our NATO allies and provide, if necessary, Canadian military forces?"[80]

Chrétien shrugged off the whole idea, believing that Canada's biggest concern was the North American security perimeter. He did not suspect that far-off Afghanistan would soon preoccupy his government, putting Canada at a crossroads and Canadians through a searching of the soul.

Canada: A Peacekeeping Nation?

The heyday of Canadian military and diplomatic clout on the international stage, though still celebrated by many Canadians, was short-lived. The intervention of Canadian Secretary of State for External Affairs, Lester Pearson in the 1956 Suez crisis, for which he won the Nobel Peace Price the following year, proclaimed Canada's reputation as a "middle power," a peacekeeping nation committed to the United Nations, multilateralism and the principle of collective security. But while successive Canadian governments sought to maintain that good reputation, together with a close military partnership with the United States, domestic matters and the protection of Canadian sovereignty against non-military threats increasingly took precedence.

After 1968 and the election of Liberal Prime Minister Pierre E. Trudeau, the Canadian military budget was cut and cut again, depleting military personnel. One of Trudeau's first political moves as Prime Minister was to announce a "comprehensive review [...] of Canada's armed forces policy, including alternative forces' structures and costing."[81] In the nuclear age a strong military made little sense to Trudeau and his close advisors; surely the money could be spent elsewhere. A complete reorganization of the armed forces was therefore undertaken and within two years the three services — ground forces, navy and air force — were unified into a single entity. The government argued that integration would save millions of dollars that could be reinvested in modern equipment, and that it would create a highly mobile and flexible force available for peacekeeping operations and "brush-fire" conflicts.

In the end the savings amounted to nothing, as they were lost to further budget cuts and inflation. As for the flexible force, it was deployed only on peacekeeping missions. "Brush-fire" conflicts were avoided at all cost.

Trudeau also announced his government's intention to "take a hard look […] at our military role in NATO and determine whether our present military commitment is still appropriate to the present situation in Europe."[82] After all it was only fair that the European allies take on more of the burden for the defense of their own continent.

In the autumn of 1968, the government chose to reduce Canada's post-war military presence in Europe. The timing was unfortunate. Just weeks earlier, the Soviet Union, with the help of its eastern European satellites, had invaded Czechoslovakia to put an end to the "Prague Spring." From then on, Ottawa's defense priorities were to be fourfold: ensuring Canadian sovereignty, contributing to North American defense, limiting commitments to the North Atlantic alliance, and peacekeeping. The new program was ambitious yet completely unrealistic.

For one thing, the issue of Canadian sovereignty was promptly dismissed as almost irrelevant since the only danger to Canada could only come from a nuclear confrontation between the United States and the Soviet Union. As tensions eased considerably after the Cuban missile crisis of 1962 and mutual nuclear deterrence helped reduce the risk of a generalized war, that possibility appeared most unlikely. As for North American defense, that remained a priority only as long as it did not require major influxes of federal cash. A Department of Defense White Paper made it clear in 1969 that the Canadian government was not "prepared to devote substantial sums to new equipment or facilities."[83] Third, in Europe, the Canadian NATO contribution, once "one of the best elements of our front line defense,"[84] was reduced to a token force of 5000 troops, under equipped and consequently uneasy about their mission.

With Canada's military commitments being so drastically reviewed, the country's peacekeeping expertise received a further boost. At first, the Trudeau government had insisted peacekeeping missions would be considered only if the prospect of success was deemed realistic. In practice, such cautionary notes never withstood the passage of time. Canadian forces became involved in a number of UN peace missions, in the Middle East, Africa and the Balkans, to name a few. For the most part, the Canadian public applauded those missions, for they could only solidify Canada's international reputation as a peaceful "helpful fixer." As Canadian historian J.L. Granastein put it, "Canadians, who like to think of themselves as especially moral and as different from the Americans, loved the attention their peacekeeping received."[85] However, this ignored three important realities.

First, the Canadian military increasingly viewed peacekeeping missions as a major hindrance, sucking up trained personnel when manpower was already scarce. The role of an army was to prepare actively for a potential war against the Soviet Union in Europe, not to help preserve peace in distant regions of the world. Second, Ottawa often saw peacekeeping missions as a necessary evil, a bargaining tool. In 1964, for instance, Canada agreed to provide troops to the UN force on the divided island of Cyprus in the Mediterranean. The arrival of Canadian troops prevented a Turkish invasion and helped maintain a fragile status quo, thus avoiding a war between Turkey and Greece, both NATO members. U.S. President Lyndon Johnson was said to be appreciative, so much so that in the following months he signed the Automotive Products Trade Agreement, also known as Auto Pact. It removed tariffs on cars and automotive parts, allowing Canada's auto sector to flourish as an integral part of the U.S. industry, in return for access to the Canadian market.[86]

Finally, the government could not repeatedly cut the defense budget without consequence. The government's seeming indifference to the needs of the armed forces was taking its toll on their sense of duty and professionalism. And on more than one occasion, dwindling resources forced the Canadian military to rely on the American partnership for logistics, airlift and equipment.

Canada's military deficiencies were bad enough during the Cold War. They grew much worse after the collapse of the Soviet bloc. The "bipolar" world, in which two rival superpowers competed on the international scene, that had dominated foreign policies since the end of the World War II was gone forever. Russia was accepted as the successor to the Soviet Union at the Security Council, mainly because it controlled strategic nuclear weapons. But, reduced to a regional power, Russia was no longer the equal of the U.S. (some historians argue that it actually never was).

The Soviet collapse sustained the idea that the West had scored a final victory, not just over Communism but over history itself. Western intellectuals wrote about the "End of History", as if we had arrived at "the end point of mankind's ideological evolution and the universalization of Western liberal democracy as the final form of human government of mankind's ideological evolution."[87] Universal peace and economic liberalism, it seemed, would soon dominate the world.

As if to acknowledge that paradigm, the Department of Foreign Affairs and International Trade released the conclusions of a full government review in 1995. Called *Canada in the World*, it identified three key goals: "the promotion of prosperity and employment, the protection of our security, within a stable global framework and the projection of Canadian values and culture." All three ideas sprang from those dominant assumptions: that good times lay ahead, that international conflicts would be small and brief, and that exporting our triumphant values would light the way to peace.

"The Government will also work to reinforce global prosperity [...] Prosperity helps to anchor international stability and enables progress towards sustainable development. More prosperous people are able to maintain more mature and mutually beneficial economic partnerships with Canada, becoming increasingly open to our values and thus more active partners in building the international system."[88]

In this new global world, "the strength of economic relations" would necessarily supersede all other considerations and help redefine international relations; or so was the widespread belief at the time. It was therefore unsurprising that "the promotion of global peace as the key to protecting our security" came second, while remaining "a central element of our foreign policy." Owing to its peacekeeping reputation, Canada seemed well positioned to promote global peace, particularly since the United Nations had finally gained a degree of relevance with the end of the Cold War.

Since 1947, Canada has participated in 72 peacekeeping and humanitarian missions[89] — nearly every single one under the auspices of the UN — from the former Yugoslavia to Rwanda and Haiti. But was it really equipped to be a global peacekeeper given its history of short-changing its Armed Forces.

Back in 1987, the Canadian government had appeared ready to break from its familiar pattern of cutting deep into military budgets, while committing to ever more missions. A Defense White Paper declared: "We will commit forces to [UN] operations if suitable resources are available, and if our personnel can be appropriately armed and properly trained to carry out the task and make a significant contribution to the success of the mission."[90] Unfortunately, those turned out to be big ifs. Brian Mulroney's Conservative government chopped the budget and entirely abandoned the replacement of obsolete land equipment such as tanks. It reduced the regular Canadian forces, while expanding peacekeeping commitments. Once again, the Army had to bear the brunt of those burgeoning obligations.

In October 1993, a federal election brought the Liberals back to power under a new leader, Jean Chrétien. In the face of a serious budget crisis, they, too, promised a complete review of Canada's military. It was time for yet another White Paper, and once again it emphasized the need "to protect the country and its citizens from challenges to their security." It concluded emphatically that "a nation not worth defending is a nation not worth preserving."[91] It also claimed that Ottawa would maintain "a multi-purpose, combat-capable armed forces able to meet the challenges to Canada's security both at home and abroad."

However, in its February 1995 budget, the government announced another round of deep cuts in military expenditures. Not only would the regular force and the reserves be diminished, but "about $15 billion worth of capital equipment will be delayed, reduced or cancelled over the next 15 years." It turned out that Canada was worth defending but only with a lot less. Meanwhile, not surprisingly, that same Liberal White Paper lauded Canada's peacekeeping and humanitarian expertise. In 1995, nearly 4 percent of "all the peacekeepers on duty in the world"[92] were Canadian, the bulk of them deployed in Bosnia.

But for all of Canada's bragging, what was the true state of its armed forces? As Condoleeza Rice wrote when she was still National Security Advisor during George W. Bush's first term: "Extended peacekeeping detracts from our readiness."[93] She might as well been describing the Canadian Army, which by the early '90s was buckling under the weight of obligations it couldn't keep. The crisis erupted in Somalia in 1993, under the auspices of a UN humanitarian intervention. Already badly overstretched, the Canadian military could only spare the Canadian Airborne Regiment (CAR), a unit trained for quick interventions but completely unprepared for long-term peacekeeping operations. As historian J.L. Granatstein observed, the CAR "seemed to be an accident waiting to happen."[94] And so it did, when a young Somali was captured, tortured and killed by two Canadian soldiers.

The Canadian Forces set up an internal board of inquiry but was bent on keeping the matter from the public eye. The country was in the midst of a federal election, and it was no time to publicize an anomalous incident caused by two troublemakers. But in the early days of 1994, a video was released to the media showing CAR soldiers tattooed with swastikas, holding bottles of beer and shouting racist and anti-Somali comments. Public condemnation came swiftly. What was happening to the proud Canadian peacekeeping tradition? How could a once elite-unite with a glorious past fall so low?

The disbanded CAR and, in 1995, appointed a Commission of Inquiry into the Deployment of Canadian forces to Somalia. Two years later, the Commission concluded that "systems broke down and organizational discipline crumbled." The root causes were identified: a lack of equipment, poor training and discipline, deficient leadership and absence of proper planning. "There seems to be little room to slide lower,"[95] the commissioners added bluntly.

The government got the message and appointed a new Chief of the Defense staff in September 1997, General Maurice Baril. Under his recommendation, Canada agreed to reduce its peacekeeping commitments. Then finally in March 2001, the Department of Defense acknowledged that the Canadian Forces, in their current strength could no longer sustain long-term commitments, peacekeeping or otherwise. The new thinking was "get in quick, get out fast." The Canadian Forces would be deployed at the outbreak of a conflict to help stabilize the "area of operation" and then be relieved. It was the exact opposite of the mission that would overtake Canada in the aftermath of 9/11.

In 2002, when Canada was forced to contemplate seriously a military deployment to Afghanistan, the fundamental problems that had plagued its Armed Forces since the late 1960s had not been solved. The morale of the army was perhaps a little higher, but the Canadian military was still under funded, poorly equipped, undermanned and over deployed.

That sad reality did not escape the Bush administration. In the fall of 2001, Paul Celluci, the American ambassador to Ottawa was instructed by the White House to address the matter with the Canadian government. The world had changed: Terrorism was now the main threat to both nations and the defense of North America a shared responsibility. Was Canada really up to the task?

Canada-US Defense Relations: The Ballistic Missile Defense

Canada and the U.S. first looked at integrating their defense during World War II. On a state visit to Canada in 1938, U.S. President Franklin Roosevelt made it clear that "the American people would not remain idle should Canadian soil be threatened of domination by another empire." Prime Minister William Lyon Mackenzie King responded in kind, declaring that Canada would never allow "enemy forces" to strike the United States from Canadian soil. A famous diarist, he even recorded that day: "I believe our defense program is doing well."[96]

Yet, despite a new rearmament program and increased military funding, the Canadian military was in no position to respond to serious threats; the Royal Canadian Air Force had only a few dozen modern aircraft at its disposal. With six destroyers in all, the Navy fared no better. As for ground troops, they were essentially comprised of poorly trained militias, with the permanent units barely reaching the 4,000 men. Washington's anxiety noticeably increased in September 1939, when Canada declared war on Germany. "It seemed to me [the President] seriously worried about our Canadian coasts being inadequately protected, a real danger for the United States," Mackenzie King wrote in the aftermath of a series of conversations with Roosevelt.[97]

Less then three weeks later, in the spring of 1940, the Germans swept through Western Europe. As Britain and her dominions fought a desperate battle for their survival, Franklin Roosevelt proposed the creation of a Permanent Joint Board on Defense. Under the dire circumstances of the day, Mackenzie King could not pass up the invitation to forge a military agreement with the U.S., thus he welcomed the arrangement as "part of the enduring foundation of a new world order, based on friendship and goodwill."

Even though the agreement defended the principle of equal participation, the economic and military weight of the United States could only favor the Americans in the long term, as Mackenzie King was all too aware. But he had made a choice: getting actively involved in the continent's defense was a better alternative than remaining on the sidelines, powerless. Another Prime Minister, John Diefenbaker, made the same choice in 1957 when he hastily agreed to the

North American Air Agreement (NORAD), which integrated the air forces of both countries under a joint command. The agreement, renamed North American Aerospace Defense Command in 1981, was renewed several times, even though the direct threat to North American security greatly diminished in the 1980s and 1990s. The Canadian government continued to believe in a continental defense because anything else would place the Americans in full control.

In the aftermath of 9/11, Washington introduced plans to deploy a ground-based ballistic missile defense (BMD). This reignited an old debate over Canada's role in securing the skies over North America. BMD had its roots in the defunct Strategic Defense Initiative of 1983, which envisioned a space-based system to fend off Soviet nuclear missiles. Then President Ronald Reagan was the project's champion, declaring on national television: "I call upon the scientific community who gave us nuclear weapons to turn their great talents to the cause of mankind and world peace: to give us the means of rendering these nuclear weapons impotent and obsolete."[98]

The grand project proved too costly to proceed, but the idea didn't die. President Bill Clinton's administration revived it because, even in the absence of the Soviet threat, the U.S. feared attacks from "rogue states" such as North Korea or Iran. Clinton wanted to focus on North American defense. Canada showed a calculated willingness to examine the idea. "[We will] examine closely those areas which may require updating in accordance with evolving challenges to continental security," and "will work towards an agreement that furthers our national interest,"[99] concluded a government White Paper in 1994.

Canada was mindful of the credibililty it had lost over the debacle in Somalia. The 1995 Commission of Inquiry had exposed very publicly the Canadian Forces' many failings. Declining outright to review the BMD program would only have tarnished Canada's already spotty credentials in Washington. Prime Minister Chrétien understood that BMD could be a political bombshell at home. Critics argued Canada was at risk of losing both its soul and it international reputation by participating in a renewed arms race. Proponents said Canada could ill afford to turn its back on continental integration, let alone its access to the lucrative U.S. defense industrial market. Therefore, the Prime Minister did everything he could to evade the potential headache of a political debate on the issue. The attacks on 9/11 put the whole project on the backburner, at least temporarily. But Ottawa needed more than ever to prove its worth in the face of terrorism. The Bush administration expected nothing less.

The Afghan Mission: Operation "Enduring Freedom" and Beyond

In the days following 9/11, the Chrétien government committed to support the U.S. in its newly formulated War on Terror. Keeping the border open was Ottawa's top priority, and to avoid seeming weak, it promised swift security enhancements. At first, no one seriously anticipated Canada would be required to participate militarily. The Canadian military leadership had long been calling for a lesser involvement in peacekeeping operations and the government was more than willing to listen. But on September 12 the UN Security Council voted unanimously resolution 1368, which condemned the attacks and called for the eradication of global terrorism. Then, on October 4, 2001, at a special press conference, the Secretary-General of NATO, George Robertson, announced that the organization was invoking the principle of article 5 of the *Treaty of Washington*. This important article states that an attack against one or several member states would automatically be considered an attack against all. As a founding member, Canada had therefore been attacked and was now obligated to play its part. A few days later, the U.S. Ambassador in Ottawa, while publicly thanking Canada for its staunch support and many gestures of sympathy at the time of the attacks, hinted his country would be expecting a military commitment from its northern ally and friend.

What form should such commitment take? The military leadership had wasted no time at debating the matter. Some argued Canadian troops should fight alongside the Americans in Kandahar, an al-Qaeda stronghold, while others recommended participation in the European-led International Security Assistance Force, a peacekeeping mission, therefore safer and more in the Canadian tradition. In the end, it was for the Prime Minister to make the final decision. As it turned out, the U.S. Secretary of Defense, Donald Rumsfeld and the White House wanted a Canadian force in Kandahar. Eager to show the greatest of support to

Washington, Ottawa agreed and on October 8, Art Eggleton, the Minister of Defense announced operation Apollo in support of operation Enduring Freedom. The mission, which involved some 800 Canadian ground troops and navy units was a departure from the more traditional peacekeeping so dear to Canadians. It was a combat mission, the first since the Korean War. In December, Canada also agreed to deploy, albeit secretly, its elite Joint Task Force 2 (JTF2). In the months to come, it was to play a key role in the overall Canadian deployment.

The Canadian Forces in Afghanistan were ready and operational by February 2002, well after the Americans had pacified the region. The government was overall satisfied, for the deployment, while relatively low-risk for the troops, could only enhance Canada's stature in Washington. Besides, the mission was not expected to last beyond six months. Beyond that point, there were no plans to stay.

Except for the tragic death of four Canadian soldiers mistakenly hit by an American laser guided bomb during training in April, the mission proved most uneventful. JTF2 did see some action but for the most part Canada's commitment to Operation Enduring Freedom remained what the decision makers in Ottawa had wanted it to be: a low-risk affair with few casualties but enough exposure to convince our American friends Canada was an active participant to the War on Terror. As John McCallum, Eagleton's replacement as Minister of Defense, paid the troops a visit in July 2002, he was confident the men in Kandahar would soon be returning home safely. He was soon to be proven wrong.[100]

In October, McCallum was invited to travel to Washington, D.C. the following month to meet with the Secretary of Defense, Donald Rumsfeld. As the crisis over Iraq was growing momentum, the purpose of the visit appeared crystal clear. Rumsfeld would want to discuss Canada's position in the face of an American invasion or perhaps continental security. McCallum flew to Washington on January 8, 2003. To his surprise, Rumsfeld entered the board room accompanied by General Richard Myers, chairman of the Joint Chiefs of Staff, the highest ranking military officer in the U.S. Armed Forces. McCallum understood at once the meeting would not be about continental security. In fact, neither Rumsfeld nor Myers was interested in talking about plans for the invasion of Iraq. A Canadian military contribution was the least of their worries. Afghanistan was to be the topic of the day. Rumsfeld bluntly asked Canada to consider maintaining military presence in Afghanistan and help stabilize and rebuild the war-torn country as the Americans would soon be focusing on Iraq.[101] The mission would remain low-risk, the Secretary of State assured McCallum, for the Taliban had been defeated. Or so he believed.

For the political establishment in Ottawa, the idea of sending more troops and even taking the lead of the NATO-led security and development mission, ISAF, in Afghanistan had one obvious advantage. Canada would be seen offering an ongoing support to the War on Terror without having to support an invasion of Iraq. Canadian military officials were of a different mindset. Canada needed to do a lot more. "Canadian Forces planners are putting everything on the table for a contribution to any war in Iraq, military sources say,"[102] declared the *National Post* on January 10, 2003. In the end, it did not really matter what the military leadership said or wished, the Prime Minister was the one to make the final call. Jean Chrétien did and two days later, McCallum announced at the House of Commons that "Canada has been approached by the international community for assistance in maintaining peace and security in Afghanistan for the UN-mandated mission in Kabul [...] We are currently in discussion with a number of potential partners."[103]

No one anticipated then that the government's new commitment to security in Afghanistan would turn into a lasting and dangerous affair. What mattered was that Canada was now off the hook. A military participation to a possible invasion of Iraq, that so many Canadians opposed, was no longer on the cards.

Iraq: The Big Divide

As the Bush administration turned its attention to Iraq, claiming that Saddam Hussein's regime not only had developed secretly weapons of mass destruction but was openly supporting terrorism, the government of Jean Chrétien grew uneasy. Surely the Americans could not expect Canada's already overstretched military to send troops to Iraq as well as Afghanistan? They did not. What Washington wanted was first and foremost a political endorsement by Canada of its aggressive stand towards Iraq. But, while Ottawa had moved swiftly to demonstrate Canada was serious in fighting terrorism at home and abroad, the government took the view the U.S. should not act unilaterally, without the full backing of the UN, to deal with Saddam Hussein's alleged weapons of mass destruction. "The Prime Minister had been saying for months that Canada was unlikely to join an invasion without explicit support from the United Nations,"[104] commented *McLean's* magazine at the end of March. Besides, even if they existed, the argument was that they did not pose an imminent threat to the security of the U.S. and its allies. All avenues of diplomacy should be contemplated first and more time should be given to the UN inspections for Iraq's alleged WMD programs. "When it became clear that the second resolution was never going to fly," recalls Jean Chrétien, "if only because France or Russia was ready to use its Security Council veto, Canada began working on a compromise that would delay invasion until [Hans] Blix had finished his work but would commit to war if he found weapons of mass destruction and Saddam refused to dismantle them."[105]

Canada's efforts at the UN to secure such a compromise failed. More importantly, those efforts were greatly resented in Washington. "How could you let us down?" Michael Kergin, the Canadian ambassador in Washington, recalled being asked on many occasions.

In the end, the Bush administration decided to proceed with its plan to invade Iraq without the UN.

What was Canada to do? Except in the Western province of Alberta, the Canadian public was decidedly hostile to the move. Then there was a provincial election going on in Quebec with the Liberals pit against the *Parti Quebecois*. No doubt the open hostility of a great majority of Quebecers to a Canadian participation in Iraq strengthened Chrétien's views on the matter. In truth, Chrétien was not prepared to support a unilateral use of force without justifiable cause. In March 2003, "a poll, conducted for the [Toronto] *Star* and the Montreal newspaper *La Presse* by EKOS Research Associates, found 71 per cent of those polled backed the decision by the Liberal government [not to support Washington's decision], with 27 per cent registering their disapproval."[106] The numbers changed somewhat in the following days, reflecting the uneasiness of some and the fear Washington's reaction might be damaging to the already strained relationship between the two countries, thus prompting an economic backlash.

The American reaction was blunt and came quickly. On March 25, Paul Cellucci, the U.S. ambassador in Canada led the charge. "So many people in the United States are so disappointed that Canada is not fully supporting us now," he said. "There is no security threat to Canada that the United States would not be ready, willing and able to help with." And when asked whether Washington might be considering punishing Canada in some ways, the ambassador replied: "It's not in our economic interests to do that [but] we'll have to wait and see if there are any ramifications."[107] Cellucci's sharp criticism, uttered with the full support of his superiors in Washington, touched a nerve and the reactions were plenty, many most unfavorable. Anti-American comments flourished, one government official going as far as calling George W. Bush "a failed statesman." But in the end, the skies did not fall upon Canada as some pundits had warned. The U.S. president cancelled his official visit to Canada to show his disappointment but the economic backlash proved minimal. Promoting retaliation measures against Canada would have been irresponsible and U.S. government officials knew it. Indeed, a few days after his speech, Cellucci called for the merging of Canadian and U.S. markets, a move that demonstrated all too clearly the strategic importance of Canada, "America's largest overall energy trading partner."[108] Despite dire predictions Washington might be tempted to make the border with Canada tighter, Cellucci announced that Canadians would be exempted from having to register with customs officials upon entering the U.S. As he pointed out, "our ties are deep and long-standing. We are dependent on each other."[109]

Canada stood firm on the Iraq issue, refusing to follow Washington's lead and sticking to its traditional principles. As former Prime Minister Chrétien concluded in his memoirs, "my real satisfaction came with knowing that we Canadians had held firm to our values as a keeper of peace through multilateral institutions, no matter how great the threats and uncertainties we faced."[110]

Chapter 4

Canada's Security Dilemma: How to Manage the Reaction to the American Reaction

In April 2004, the then-incoming Paul Martin government released the document *"Securing an Open Society: Canada's National Security Policy,"* arguably the first document on Canada's national security, "a strategic framework and action plan designed to ensure that Canada is prepared for and can respond to current and future threats."[111] Did it help clarify Canada's position on the U.S.-led War on Terror? Not particularly, given that the War on Terror is not even mentioned! However, the Canadian government website is clear on one thing: the document "has been crafted to balance the needs for national security with the protection of core Canadian values of openness, diversity and respect for civil liberties."

Beyond that, the National Security Policy remains fairly vague as to what it seeks to accomplish. In its preamble, Prime Minister Martin takes great pains to put the focus on national security threats to Canada such as "the recent SARS outbreak and the 2003 electrical blackout [...] and more longstanding threats [...] organized crime and natural disasters."[112]

Obviously by avoiding all references to the War on Terror, the government was aligning itself with Canadian public opinion. It was essential to present a document promoting a strictly "Made in Canada" approach to "security threats", whatever they may be, even those quite removed from terrorism. This was despite increasing pressure from the U.S. and even at home to embrace further continental harmonization. It was, of course, a huge political calculation by Martin: he could ill-afford to be seen as a blind follower of Washington's costly global war against terrorism, yet he had to signal that Canada was serious in fighting international terror. Besides, the Canadian public's attention to terrorist threats and security issues had greatly diminished since 9/11.

"The Martin security agenda creates great expectations,"[113] *The Globe and Mail* commented in December 2003, days after the new Prime Minister had been sworn in and a few weeks before *"Securing an Open Society"* was released. Less than two years later, Martin's progress on matters of national security was generally acknowledged despite "a noticeable slackening of pace"[114] after the June 2004 federal election, which had reduced the Liberals to a minority government. "The broad outlines of initiatives [...] represent an assertive attempt to design a "Made in Canada" policy, despite pressures both from within Canada and from the United States to pursue harmonization with American paradigms for homeland security and the War on Terror."[115]

Since 2006, the Conservative government of Stephen Harper has followed the course, promising to invest billions of dollars in the Canadian Forces to better prepare them for the challenges they face in Afghanistan. The Conservatives had pledged a "Canada First" security policy that would focus on continental integration with the U.S., but in fact, the mission in Afghanistan has superseded those domestic issues and become Canada's major contribution to the War on Terror was concerned.

Securing an Open Society: A New Era for Security Issues in Canada

Paul Martin, formerly Chrétien's Minister of Finance, took office on December 12, 2003, having won the leadership of the ruling Liberal party. In the preceding months, as his leadership campaign had unfolded, Martin had called for far-reaching organizational changes within the government and a new course of action in matters of national security and defense. For all its commitment to introduce extensive changes, the Chrétien cabinet never saw the benefits of an overall policy framework. Paul Martin was willing to provide a detailed blueprint for action against potential threats to Canada. He also promised relations with the U.S. would greatly improve under his watch. It was now time to act.

The first sign of a clean break from the Chrétien days was the complete revamping of the Cabinet, as new faces appeared and ministers with minor portfolios were promoted. Notable exceptions were Bill Graham, who remained the Minister of Foreign Affairs, and Ann

McLellan, the former Justice Minister, who became Deputy Prime Minister.

David Pratt's ascension to Minister of National Defense was arguably the most symbolic of the new appointments. As the only Liberal MP to have supported both a Canadian intervention in Iraq and the U.S. Ballistic Missile Defense system, Pratt firmly believed Canada-U.S. relations ought to be stronger and Ottawa more open to continental integration. He had expertise in military and defense issues, and as chair of a parliamentary committee on military expenditures, Pratt had recommended billions of dollars in new defense spending, leading many pundits to believe that the Canadian Armed Forces would finally get overdue attention and funding. "Pratt knows there must be an enormous investment in the Canadian Forces and that, without such expenditures, Canada will be without the capability of conducting a foreign policy, let alone a military one,"[116] wrote an enthusiastic defense analyst.

The appointment of McLellan as deputy Prime Minister was yet another signal that national security was to take centre stage. The lone Liberal MP from the province of Alberta and a long-time supporter of Martin's Prime Ministerial ambitions, McLellan had been a strong proponent of national security since 9/11. As Justice Minister under Chrétien, she had presided over the implementation of new anti-terrorist and security legislation, particularly bill C-36. She was, therefore, a logical choice to supervise the massive bureaucratic reorganization that Paul Martin had in mind. She was concurrently appointed minister of a brand new Department of Public Safety and Emergency

Preparedness - the equivalent of the U.S. Department of Homeland Security - "responsible for the protection of the public and the maintenance of a just, peaceful and safe society."[117]

In effect, McLellan was to oversee and coordinate a wide range of government agencies responsible for intelligence, national security and the management of border issues, all through a central hub known as Government Operation Centre (GOC).[118] Its primary function is "to provide coordination and direction on behalf of the federal government" as a crisis, national or international, is unfolding, while maintaining close contacts with Canada's provinces and territories, as well as its international partners. The GOC also keeps a list of "entities" allegedly associated with terrorism and is responsible for issuing "security certificates" to individuals who present a grave risk to national security, whatever that may be, thus forcing them to house arrest, jail time or deportation. Five of those certificates have been issued since 2001.[119]

But, as much as U.S. Homeland Security had focused primarily on the war against terrorism, the new ministry was to encompass "government-wide responses to *all* emergencies, including public health, natural disasters and security." In keeping with its proposed "all threats" strategy, the government promised to set up a Public Health Agency to "address public health risks and coordinate a national response to health crises."

Within days, the Prime Minister also announced the creation of two cabinet committees, one on Global

Affairs and the other on Canada-U.S. Relations to "help promote an integrated approach across government to Canada-U.S. issues," which he intended on chairing. At the time, the media took little notice that Martin was placing so much importance on improving relations with the U.S. His impetus was primarily economic. Several trade disputes, including a simmering battle over softwood lumber, continued to taint relations. In May 2002, the U.S. government had imposed hefty customs duties on Canadian softwood lumber, accusing Canada of unfair subsidies. Then in the spring of 2003, veterinary officials in the province of Alberta warned of a potential, albeit isolated, case of mad cow disease, prompting Washington to close the border to Canadian beef.

To make matters worse, the outbreak of SARS in 2003 was followed a few months later by the Northeast Electrical Blackout, a massive power outage that originated from New York State (contrary to initial rumors that Canada was somehow responsible.) Months later, the terrorist attacks on commuter trains in Madrid somehow seemed to punctuate Canada's perceived inadequacies in matters of continental security, not least at home.

In her report entitled "National Security in Canada — the 2001 Anti-Terrorism initiative," tabled in the House of Commons in March 2004, Canada's Auditor General, Sheila Fraser, found "a lack of coordination among security agencies" and troubling weaknesses in information sharing. "Overall," the report concluded, "these gaps and deficiencies point to a requirement to strengthen the management framework for security and intelligence. Improvement is especially needed in the management of issues that cross agency boundaries, such as information systems, watch lists, and personnel screening."[120] A Senate Standing Committee on National Security and Defense, chaired by Senator Colin Kenny, released two scathing reports on coastal and airport security and emergency preparedness: "The Myth of Security at Canada's Airports" in January 2003 and "Canada's Coastlines: The Longest Under-Defended Borders in the World" in October.

Both Fraser's conclusions and the Kenny Committee's reports appeared damning at the time. All three opposition parties — the New Democrats, the Conservatives and the separatist *Bloc Québecois* — wasted no time in criticizing a security policy they saw as completely inadequate. But their interest in matters of national security was intermittent at best. They certainly failed to offer a common front, with the Conservatives demanding further continental integration and the New Democrats denouncing integration as a threat to Canadian sovereignty. Analysts and intellectuals also took potshots at Ottawa. In her book, Jennifer Welsh refers to the Auditor General's "report on the failure of federal government departments to collaborate on counterterrorism and emergency response."[121]

However, with a disturbing unanimity, the pundits, political or otherwise, failed to consider that Fraser's and the Senate Committee's reports were mere retrospectives of past actions and policies, not an outright condemnation. At a press conference, Ms.

Fraser was quick to point out that, although the government of Canada still had a lot of work to do, many of her recommendations had been or were in the process of being met and "that Canada's performance in managing national security in the past two and a half years is consistent with that of our international peers. Other countries, including the United States, have examined similar areas and have reported findings comparable with those of our audit."[122] As for the Kenny Committee, a 2004 update, while warning that "given the serious gaps outstanding, closing our books on these issues would constitute negligence on [our] part," concluded that "the federal government has made progress in dealing with Canada's […] security shortcomings over the past year."[123]

The Martin government took little comfort from either the Auditor-General's remarks or, later that year, from the Kenny Committee's encouraging update. Further policy changes in all matters of security and intelligence were urgently required, if only to bring about a more integrated system "fully connected to key partners — provinces, territories, communities, first-line responders, the private sector and Canadians." On the heels of the Fraser report and to "respond to [the] increasingly complex and dangerous threat environment," Ottawa promptly introduced Canada's very first national security policy: *Securing an Open Society: Canada's National Security Policy.*

Canada's "Three Core National Security Interests"

"I hope it is not just to please the United States that, this morning, the government is making this statement on a new security policy,"[124] commented *Bloc Québecois* MP Yvan Loubier, revealing in the process that Canada's Minister of Finance had discussed the policy with U.S. Treasury Secretary John Snow a few days prior. Was the Canadian government so eager to obtain Washington's approval of its new policy that it would approach the U.S. administration first, even before presenting it to Parliament? It certainly looked that way to the media. For instance, CTV News was quick to point out "the announcement is seen as a goodwill gesture to the United States, just days before Prime Minister Paul Martin is due to head to Washington to meet U.S. President George Bush. Martin has been eager to reassure the Bush administration that Canada is taking domestic security as seriously as the United States."[125]

The U.S. government certainly expressed its satisfaction at such a decisive move. "It sounded to me very much like what we were doing, so I applauded the development,"[126] declared Treasury Secretary Snow. President Bush also welcomed the "series of critical steps to guard against the danger of terrorism," and later that year he felt moved to praise "the government [of Canada] for all [its] constructive and important decisions."[127] Canada had finally created its own Department of Homeland Security to respond effectively to national security threats, or so it seemed.

Both Snow and Bush were wrong in their belief that Canada's new security strategy was a mere copycat of their own interpretation of "national security." Contrary to *National Security Strategy of the United States of America*, or the Bush Doctrine, *"Securing an Open Society"* was never designed as an offensive strategy focused solely on the threat of terrorism. As a possible terrorist target, Canada naturally understands the need to enhance security within its territory and has sought to calm Washington's concerns, primarily to protect vital economic ties. But — and this is a fundamental aspect of Ottawa's approach to security matters — Canadian governments since 2001 have resisted an American-style security strategy and consistently refused to join in a North American security perimeter, putting forward a "made in Canada" approach.

The document defines Canada's "three core national security interests: protecting Canada and Canadians at home and abroad; ensuring Canada is not a base for threats to our allies; contributing to international security."[128] We must review each of those interests to understand the fundamentals. "Protecting Canada and Canadians at home and abroad" referred in large part to a better control of immigration flows into the country and the enhancement of border security. "The National Security Policy calls for the development of the next generation of the Smart Border agenda, which could also engage Mexico in strengthening our shared security, building economic prosperity and protecting the health and safety of our citizens,"[129] declared Ann McLellan.

The Canada-U.S. Smart Border Declaration, signed in December 2001, had helped to establish a "zone of confidence against terrorist activity."[130] The collapse of the Soviet Union in 1991 and China's conversion to a more open economy had appeared to confirm the triumph of liberalism on a global scale, the utter victory of the "free world" against communism. Growing economic interdependence spawned a conventional wisdom that borders had become obsolete and were little more than a hindrance to the natural flow of goods and people. "President Vicente Fox of Mexico epitomized this view at the regional level by entering office promoting a bold vision of an open U.S.-Mexico border, including the free movement of labor, and the creation of a North American community."[131] Following the 9/11 attacks, however, borders came back in style with a vengeance. Canada could not remain on the sidelines, given the U.S. fixation on preventing another attack. "Some nations need to be more vigilant against terrorism at their borders if they want their relationship with the U.S. to remain the same,"[132] said U.S. Secretary of State Colin Powell. It was clear that the U.S. was determined to protect its borders, in cooperation with its two neighbors, Canada and Mexico, or unilaterally if necessary.

Under considerable pressure from Washington, the subsequent initiatives made "both countries partners in systems and programs that expedite the flow of low-risk goods and people while increasing the information that is needed to screen higher-risk flows."[133] They included the NEXUS program, designed to allow "low risk" individuals to cross the border faster by using an identification card obtained through an interview and finger printing process, and the Free and Secure Trade (FAST) program. Considered even more a priority, the FAST program focused on securing the flow of commerce across the border. All major crossings were to be equipped with designated fast lanes to facilitate the clearance of pre-registered participants identified as low-risk. Such initiatives could not have been entirely successful without significant investments in border and port infrastructure. As the Bush administration announced $2.1 billion USD in additional spending to better secure the 49th parallel,[134] Ottawa was prompt to commit to $1.2 billion CAD in infrastructure funding and established a Border Infrastructure Fund specifically to support the Smart Border initiatives.

Though the initial impetus for the Smart Border agreements was to limit the negative impact on the Canadian economy, over time they proved to be a resounding success for Ottawa. "There was a huge potential for countries like the U.S. and Canada to turn inward after 9/11 and to let fear dominate our public policy-making. But this would have been a huge gift to terrorists. Instead, we showed the world how to build a twenty-first century border."[135]

The Martin government sought to move the Smart Border strategy into a new and more ambitious phase, one that not only included the full participation of Mexico but envisioned the internationalization of the concept. Since the idea had been a success, why not extend it to other major powers in the world? The harmonization of policies between the U.S. and Canada did not stop there. Immigration remained a primary concern. The Canada-U.S. Safe Third Country Agreement, a joint program aimed at better managing the flow of refugee claimants, took effect in December 2002. Refugee-advocacy groups have long criticized the measure but to no avail. Paul Martin was determined to stay the course: "The government will tackle new measures to streamline our refugee determination process to ensure efficient protection for people genuinely in need and to facilitate effective removals of people attempting to abuse our refugee program."[136]

In essence, the proposed policies bore contradictions for they would necessarily work against those same "Canadian interests" the government swore to defend. As discussed in chapter 2, Canada increasingly relies on immigration to sustain its economic growth, and enhanced security at the borders automatically brings about a more profound integration of policies and practices with the United States; this raises the second "core interest," ensuring that Canadian territory does not become a base for threats to our traditional allies, and more specifically to the United States. As we have seen, even before the tragic events of 9/11, Canada was dismissed as a weak link in the fight against terrorism and a possible haven for terrorists. Canadian governments have repeatedly attempted to curb that image. McLellan proposed, if rather vaguely, that better intelligence derived through more concerted efforts was the answer. "The government will create a new Integrated Threat Assessment Centre that will comprise representatives from across the security and intelligence community and will have access to all sources of information on possible threats to Canada,"[137] she proposed. A deeper integration of policies with the United States remains essential to achieving success. The establishment of an Integrated Border Enforcement Team program (IBETS), a critical component within the Smart Border Declaration exemplifies such integration; with its mandate to enhance "integrity and security at the Canada/United States border by identifying, investigating and interdicting persons and organizations which pose a threat to national security or are engaged in other organized criminal activity"[138].

In the long run, Canada was prepared to reconsider the role it was willing — or needed — to play in the global War on Terror by acknowledging a simple yet fundamental reality: national security threats are global and can only be contained through effective prevention and the integration of resources. "The integrated threat assessment must be connected to an effective, tactical capability to deploy resources in proportionate response to specific situations, and communicate relevant information to first line responders such as the law enforcement community."[139]

But integration and convergence of policies never meant that Canada's understanding of national security threats should be identical to Washington's. Indeed, one of the most interesting aspects of "*Securing an Open Society*" is that Canada's approach to national security threats are fundamentally different from Washington's. The document starts by reminding Canadians that security issues are nothing new and that, over the years, governments "have managed a wide range of threats to our society — from the influenza epidemic of 1918-19 to the risk posed by

Soviet bombers that led to the creation of NORAD." Then it goes on defining security threats by not limiting them to terrorist attacks, whatever the form they may take. This is a fundamental departure from the Bush administration's rather narrow approach to national security. Indeed, the document considers a wider range of threats, from natural disasters to critical infrastructure vulnerability to pandemics. "The recent SARS outbreak and the 2003 electrical blackout show how our interconnectedness to events generated elsewhere can have a major impact on the health and well-being of Canadians." The failure to mention terrorism reflected Canada's reality. As Canadian professor Reg Whitaker argued, "From the point of view of measurable damage, from loss of life to severe economic costs, these latter threats have in practice been far more destructive of Canadian interests than terrorism, which has, to date, left this country directly untouched since 9/11."[140]

Ottawa's approach was also presented as a far better strategy to deal with issues of national security. Barely a few days after *Securing an Open Society* had been tabled by the government, fate provided a timely example. A bird landed on a power line at the Los Angeles airport, causing a blackout and disrupting air traffic for hours. A few days later, James Woolsey, former CIA director under Bill Clinton and a staunch proponent of Bush's pre-emptive strategy in Iraq, commented on the "sensitivity to small events [that] is a an integral feature of all complex, interconnected systems." He argued that such interdependence necessarily presented the world with new "malignant" threats as opposed to "malevolent" ones, for instance a terrorist attack using biological weapons. (Another example of a "malignant" threat would be the recent outbreak of "swine flu" and the risks of global pandemic.) "We may be tempted to treat malignant threats as long-term problems and malevolent threats as pressing — but the distinction is false. We don't get to choose between dealing with one or the other. Both can cause catastrophic damage. And one can exacerbate the other, by design or coincidence."[141]

The threat of biological weapons certainly cannot be underestimated, but focusing solely on terrorist threats might lead to failure, as demonstrated by the tremendous difficulties the U.S. government encountered, in 2002, when it launched a national campaign of vaccination against smallpox in the event of a bioterrorist attack. Not only did medical experts warn about the vaccine's potentially lethal side effects, but after years of cutbacks, the U.S. public health system appeared unable to carry out the task at hand. "Analyzing what went wrong with the civilian program, insiders and outsiders point in part to the government's mistakes and in part to the political and even psychological resistance of the doctors and nurses who were meant to carry out the vaccinations," read an editorial of the *Washington Post*. The administration focused on the stockpiling of smallpox vaccines but failed to consult with the medical community, health workers and hospital administrators and doctors. Already short of staff, hospitals were reluctant to embrace a campaign that would have proved an additional financial burden. As the editorial concluded, "Stockpiling vaccines is not enough if people are not willing to use them."[142]

The approach in Canada has been far different. Instead of thinking only within the parameters of a terrorist threat and preparing exclusively for possible bioterrorist attacks, Ottawa has considered its public health system to be a cornerstone of its national security preparedness. The system was designed to ensure that all residents "have reasonable access to medically necessary hospital and physician services, on a prepaid basis."[143] The SARS crisis of 2003 outlined the system's many weaknesses, particularly the lack of communication between various levels of government, not to mention a disturbing shortage of health resources. The government learned a great deal from that crisis, and it should therefore come as no surprise that an entire section of *"Securing an Open Society"* discusses public health emergencies. A Public Health Agency was thus created, a chief public health officer appointed and a National Microbiology Laboratory, located in Winnipeg, with 400 employees, designated as "one of the handful of laboratories in the world with the capacity to work with highly pathogenic viruses." The laboratory has been playing an active role in the H1N1 flu virus outbreak, developing a test aimed at determining the exact nature of the new strain of influenza, completing the full genome sequencing of the virus, and thus contributing significantly to a global better understanding of its possible impacts.[144]

The third "core interest" is perhaps the most ambitious of all, if anything because it is so hazy. What does "contributing to international security" mean exactly? Military intervention? Deeper integration with international law enforcement? Or improving Canada's intelligence system? All three, one might argue. The

Martin government's credibility on the issue of "international security" was soon put to the test.

The Ballistic Missile Defense (BMD) Initiative... Again!

During his campaign for the Liberal leadership, Paul Martin had made it quite clear that he would seriously consider joining the Bush administration's Ballistic Missile Defense initiative, yet another departure from the Chrétien days. "I certainly don't want to see Canada isolated from any moves that the United States might take to protect the continent," Martin had said back in April 2003 on CTV's *Question Period*. But, while the Department of National Defense strongly recommended such a move, the Ministry of Foreign Affairs continued to show a great deal of skepticism. In 2002, the House of Commons Foreign Affairs Committee had warned that "the Government should not make a decision about missile defense systems being developed by the United States, as the technology has not been proven and details of deployment are not known."[145]

Once in power, Martin had to decide whether Canada should join or reject the Bush administration initiative, and quickly, for there was a growing sense of urgency. In the U.S. Bush was campaigning for reelection with the promise of a workable system by the end of 2004. In Canada, the proponents of ballistic defense seized the opportunity to go on the offensive, arguing that the country's existing missile protection was at risk if Canada demurred. They said the proposed Missile Defense system would necessarily rely on detection and the tracking of information, until then provided through the Canada-US continental North American Aerospace Defense (NORAD); they said Canada's non-participation would lead Washington to abandon NORAD altogether. Diplomatically, this would constitute a major setback, as Ottawa inevitably would be relegated to the sidelines of continental defense. In the post-9/11 era, that was not an acceptable option.

As months passed, it became clear the Bush administration was determined to press forward with its missile initiative, with or without Canada. For the Martin government, the problematic should have been simple enough: would greater cooperation in the area of missile defense fall within the scope of Ottawa's new national security agenda? And would BMD effectively protect Canadians?

The Cold War may have officially ended in 1991 with the final collapse of the Soviet Union, but the threat of ballistic missile attacks remains. Although it is highly improbable that Russia or China would consider flexing their nuclear muscles in the current international context, they still have the capability of launching warheads against North America. However, BMD, which had begun in 1998 under the Clinton administration, was never intended to protect North America against a renewed Russian or Chinese threat. It was planned as a shield against the rise of "rogue states," the actions of terrorist cells and the proliferation of weapons of mass destruction.[146] "Although the ballistic missile threat to Canada is not currently considered to be high, joint Canadian and American intelligence estimates suggest that in the coming years the range and accuracy of ballistic missile technology available to potential proliferators will improve, weapons of mass destruction proliferation will continue and the threat to Canada and Canadian interests could increase."[147]

But here's the thing: even if those "rogue states" — North Korea and Iran immediately come to mind — are in a position to develop long-range missiles capable of threatening North America, it will take years before the missile shield can be operational. Numerous reports suggested that BMD was a gamble, one report in particular from the U.S. General Accounting Office, the non-partisan, independent investigative arm of Congress, the equivalent of the Auditor General in Canada. It said the Missile Defense project had experienced delays and suffered budget shortfalls to the extent that "comprehensive assessments of the capabilities and limitations of the [ballistic missile defense system] are not currently possible."[148] In other words, despite the ambitious timetable set by George W. Bush, the system offered no protection whatsoever against missile threats. Therefore, was Canadian support really paramount?

The U.S. ambassador in Canada, Paul Cellucci, seemed to believe it was, and he was irritated by the Chrétien government's non-committal stance. Throughout 2003, he had urged Ottawa to make up its mind on participating. NORAD's future was at stake, he warned. Besides, Canada's refusal to back the American-led coalition in Iraq had already angered a large part of official Washington. In that light, Canada was being offered a golden opportunity to send a strong and positive message to the Bush administration. Canadian officials were still very much divided on the issue, with many Liberal MPs opposed to a scheme associated with an all-too-unpopular U.S. administration. In the end, Chrétien agreed only to open informal discussions with the U.S. They had barely begun when Paul Martin became Prime Minister.

His Defense Minister, David Pratt, was prompt to establish contact with U.S. Secretary of Defense Donald Rumsfeld. Pratt wrote to him: "It is our intent to negotiate in the coming months a Missile Defense Framework Memorandum of Understanding with the United States with the objective of including Canada as a participant in the current U.S. missile defense program and expanding and enhancing information exchange."[149] As it turned out, Canada's good intentions served no particular purpose. Not only did the "discussions" achieve nothing but U.S. officials proved reticent about sharing information with their Canadian counterparts. A few months and a federal election later, the Liberal majority found itself reduced to a minority, and the Prime Minister was no longer prepared to support BMD unequivocally. The file had become highly controversial, particularly in the province of Quebec, where the Liberals were already struggling. In the meantime, as Bush was running for a second term, opinion polls found that a strong majority of Canadians believed America was no longer Canada's strongest ally and friend. Bush's re-election in November 2004 with a majority of the popular vote and Republican control of both the House of

Representatives and the Senate did not augur well for Canada-U.S. relations.

Unfortunately for Paul Martin, Canada's participation in BMD was to remain a hot issue for some time. Following his victory, George W. Bush made a long-overdue visit to Canada in December 2004. Canadian officials had impressed upon the White House that it would be counterproductive for the president to discuss BMD publicly during his visit. Instead, following a meeting with Paul Martin, Bush called on the Canadian government to agree to his missile program. "We talked about the future of NORAD and how that organization can best meet emerging threats and safeguard our continent against attack from ballistic missiles," Bush said at the press conference. "I hope we'll also move forward on ballistic missile defense cooperation to protect the next generation of Canadians and Americans from the threats we know will arise."[150]

Martin was reportedly furious. BMD was once again at the forefront of political debate. To add insult to injury, developments on the home front had forced the precarious Liberals, clinging to power, to align themselves with the New Democrats, a party prone to attacking BMD. In the following weeks, the NDP and the Bloc Québecois went on the offensive, accusing the government of supporting a program that would force Russia and China to rebuild their respective nuclear arsenals, thus paving the way to a new arms race. They reminded the Prime Minister that Canada's approach was to promote multilateral arms control mechanisms, not to involve the country in a project that would put weapons in space. Martin was accused of being most indecisive on the issue by all opposition parties, including the Conservatives who supported Canada's participation. (A few months later, the magazine *The Economist* would dub Martin "Mr. Dithers" for his reputation for indecisiveness on other issues.)

As the attacks increased in intensity and the media focused in on BMD, the tensions within the Liberal caucus at the House of Commons were palpable. The minority government could fall at any time and the Liberals could not hope to win a majority without Quebec. "The Quebec wing of the party will submit a resolution urging Martin to turn down the Bush administration's invitation to participate in the shield," commented Quebec journalist Chantal Hébert, "Quebec is a key piece of the puzzle to ensure a Liberal election majority. It is also a hotbed of opposition to missile defense."[151]

In the end, the very survival of the government and the possibility of yet another federal election forced the Prime Minister to come up with a decision on BMD: Canada would not participate in the negotiation of a North American Missile Defense system after all. As much as he had favored a better relationship with the U.S., Martin's main priority was to remain at the helm. Washington received advance warning of Canada's decision to reject participation. The public announcement was made on February 25, 2005. The Canadian government expected the Americans to express displeasure, but instead their reaction was muted. George W. Bush took his time to call the Prime Minister and discuss the matter of BMD, as if Ottawa's decision was of little consequence. In truth, Canada's refusal to join the missile program would not prevent the Bush administration from pursuing a policy it felt was necessary to protect Americans from nuclear threats. Canada was not needed. Paul Martin's government had gone a long way to align itself with Bush's America, even though full participation in BMD would have done little to address Canada's core security interests. Ironically, that includes the goal of ensuring that Canadian policies do not threaten the security of our main ally and neighbor. In the end, political opposition at home forced the government to reconsider its initial support.

However, despite the appearance that U.S. officials had shrugged off Canada's decision, there was still trepidation that the close relationship between the two countries had suffered considerable damage, perhaps irreparable damage. Something had to be done to show that Canada was not a loose cannon and was serious about the global fight against international terrorism. After Iraq and BMD, the only logical intervention was Afghanistan.

The Afghan Challenge: Canada's Mission to End in 2011?

A little over two weeks before the Canadian government announced officially it was rejecting BMD, Bill Graham, now Defense minister, had appointed General Rick Hillier as Chief of the Defense Staff.

Formerly in command of the NATO-led International Security Assistance Force in Afghanistan, Hillier was known for challenging Ottawa on the sad state of the Canadian Forces and calling for an increase in military funding. "In this country, we could probably not give enough resources to the men and women to do all the things that we ask them to do," he very publicly told Graham and the Prime Minister on the day of his appointment. "But we can give them too little, and that is what we are now doing. Remember them in your budgets."[152] Funding was all the more necessary now that the reality of warfare had dramatically changed, he believed. What Canada needed was a well-equipped, small but efficient army in a position to face with its traditional allies new global threats, from rogue states to terrorist organizations. The notion of "rogue state" or failed state, depending on the vocabulary used, was central to Hillier's vision. By definition, in the post Cold War era, a failed state is bound to generate regional instability and breed terrorism, thus presenting a broader threat to the international community. He referred to the concept of the "Three-Block War" to illustrate the simultaneous challenges the Canadian military should prepare for: peacekeeping operations, humanitarian relief and combat. "In order to address these security challenges, the Government is setting a new course for the Canadian Forces," he wrote in a Defense Policy Statement. "The recent operational experience of our military and the threats we are likely to face in the future point to the need for a bold vision."[153] One of the "threats" was to be found in Afghanistan, where Hillier believed Canada should play a more decisive role. Just a few weeks earlier, his proposal to send more troops to the war-torn country would have been rapidly dismissed both by Foreign Affairs and the Department of National Defense as unrealistic, costly and politically unwise. However, Canada's rejection of BMD had changed the whole situation. Hillier's arrival coincided with the emergence of a new consensus in Ottawa: Canada had to intensify its military contribution in Afghanistan to dissipate any doubt it was willing to play a significant role in the war against international terrorism and, of course, to repair the relationship with the United States following the BMD refusal.

Between October 2001 and the present, the Canadian deployment in Afghanistan has encompassed three main phases: initially in support of U.S.-led Operation Enduring Freedom, to help root out the Taliban after the fall of the regime; then from September 2003 until the spring of 2005, a second strong military deployment as part of the NATO-led ISAF mission around the Afghan capital, Kabul; and, finally a military presence in the more dangerous Kandahar region, which is ongoing, for which Hillier's influence proved essential.

By the winter of 2005, as NATO appeared committed to widen its Afghan mandate to secure the whole of Afghanistan, the Canadian government made it known it was open to the idea of deploying a 220 person Provincial Reconstruction Team (PRT) in Kandahar. Although it was to include officials from the Canadian International Development Agency (CIDA), the federal agency whose mandate it is to fight poverty and help improve political and economic conditions in poor states, the RCMP and Foreign Affairs, the military aspect of the mission as it was proposed was undeniable. Priorities included helping to bolster Afghan policing in the region, promoting security and participating in the reconstruction efforts. Given the strong presence of the Taliban in Kandahar, the mission would carry greater risks than any previous deployment. Yet General Hillier wanted to go even further.

In addition to the PRT, he favored the deployment of JTF2 Special Forces, a strong gesture that could only please Washington, given its focus on Iraq and its urgent need to secure the still-unstable situation in Afghanistan, and a regular combat force of at least 800 men. Reconstruction and stabilization were therefore the key elements of a future Canadian intervention in the Kandahar region. But stabilization of that part of Afghanistan meant the Canadian Forces would have to be involved in direct combat and casualties were to be expected, a marked change from the traditional notion of Canadian peacekeeping interventions since the Korean War.[154]

As if to prepare the public for such shift, officials in Ottawa, both civilian and military, refrained from using the word *war* when they discussed Hillier's plan. No one at that point anticipated the Taliban's strength. The Prime Minister's approval was of course needed. At the helm of a minority government, Paul Martin was anxious to avoid any political backlash at a time when the Bush administration policies had sunk to new levels of unpopularity in Canada. It was essential that Canada not be perceived as merely following Washington's strategy. So Martin took his time in giving Foreign

Affairs and the Department of Defense a response to Hillier's. For a while, he seemed to support the notion of an intervention in the Darfur, where Canada would lead international relief in its pure tradition of peacekeeping. "This kind of action helps our sense of well-being as a country," he admitted. "Our military policy should support that."[155] But it was said there would be no intervention in the Darfur, for Paul Martin's Cabinet eventually agreed to Hillier's plan.

By the time Stephen Harper and his Conservatives won a minority government in January 2006, Canada had been playing a major role in one of Afghanistan's most dangerous region for nearly six months. The Canadian military presence had grown to a 2,500-person combat force; the mission of reconstruction and stabilization had quickly evolved into a full blown war against Taliban insurgents. It was a very different kind of war! Canadian troops have had to adapt traditional military strategies in order to fight strong, constantly moving pockets of Taliban resistance determined to drive away the western presence.

Insurgency in Afghanistan relies on two key components. The first is known in military jargon as "asymmetrical" warfare, whereby small groups engage well equipped and trained conventional armies by the simplest and cheapest methods — suicide attacks or nighttime operations, for instance — thus compensating for their military inferiority. Second, the insurgency relies on political support from local populations. To complicate matters further, Afghanistan lucrative narcotics trade is known to help fund the Taliban insurgents. The eradication of poppy crops — from which heroin is derived — would seem to be an obvious goal but it has proven difficult to achieve. The Taliban offer protection to farmers frustrated from losing their main source of income, transforming them into potential fresh recruits. Canadian commanders on the ground remained confident, however. "We will persevere," Brig.-Gen. David Fraser told reporters upon taking command of the Canadian Forces in Kandahar. "We'll lean into this mission and make sure that we are successful because at the end of the day, it's important that Afghans have a secure environment that they can go and take for granted what you and I take for granted here."[156]

And persevere was what Canadian troops were expected to do under the new government. Barely three months in his tenure, Harper, despite the daunting difficulties facing Canadian troops in the Kandahar region, called for an extension of the Afghan mission until 2009, which was promptly and with little debate put to a vote at the House of Commons. To this day, it is unclear what drove the freshly elected Prime Minister to deal so hastily with Canada's involvement in Afghanistan. What is clear, however, is that the Conservative government was willing to go further than the previous government, now that counter-insurgency missions were required.

In the summer of 2006, as the Taliban directly threatened the city of Kandahar, Canadian Forces participated in NATO's Operation Medusa to stop them. After two weeks of heavy fighting, the operation was hailed "a significant success." "The ability of the Taliban to stay and fight in groups is finished," boasted the governor of the Kandahar province. "The enemy has been crushed."[157] The truth, of course, was less promising. Yes, the Canadians had prevented the Taliban from capturing Kandahar, which could then have been used as the starting point of a broader offensive against the Afghan government. Yes, the Taliban had indeed been driven back but they were far from defeated. But many insurgents were able to escape and regroup. And the fighting went on.

Back home, the debate over the Canadian mission in Afghanistan intensified. After years of relative indifference, as the situation on the ground appeared to deteriorate at a fast pace and casualties mounted with no end of the fighting in sight, the Canadian public started to re-evaluate the whole mission. In the first half of 2006, support for the Afghan mission dropped below 50 percent. At the beginning of August, Stephen Harper vowed to stay the course. "For those who have lost their family or their colleagues, these are always terrible moments," he said. "As fellow Canadians, I know that we all share their grief. But what the men and women in harm's way want and need to know in moments like this is that their government and Canadians stand behind their missions." An Ipsos-Reid poll released a few days later showed 52 percent of respondents believed the troops should be brought home swiftly.[158]

The government certainly felt the heat and, by October 2007, the Prime Minister called for an independent panel under the leadership of former Liberal deputy primer minister, John Manley to make recommendations. The Manley Report, as it came to be known, was released just three months later. It recommended that Canada maintain a presence in Afghanistan but on several conditions: other NATO members must firmly commit to bring an additional 1,000 soldiers into the region; better equipment must be supplied to protect the troops on the ground; and, ultimately, the mission should shift its emphasis from combat to diplomacy and reconstruction.[159]

Seven weeks later, a government motion calling for Canadian troops to remain in Afghanistan beyond 2009, but with a pre-determined pull-out in 2011, passed easily in the House of Commons. Since then, the government of Stephen Harper has repeated its pledge to bring troops home in 2011, but it might prove difficult to entirely switch the focus to diplomacy or humanitarianism. As U.S. President Barack Obama prepares to withdraw troops from Iraq, he has called for a "surge" in Afghanistan and renewed NATO efforts. Although the Canadian mission in Afghanistan past 2011 was not discussed when Obama visited Ottawa in February 2009, there is little doubt the question will re-emerge in the next few months. Already some military analysts expect Canadian troops to remain in Afghanistan "in a reconfigured mission focusing on training and security."[160] Considering Canada's close ties with the United States, the two countries' integrated economies and Washington's ongoing focus on security issues, Ottawa may have no choice but to recommit to having a primary combat role. The challenges in terms of cost, military strategy and overall foreign policy would daunting — all the more so given that many Canadians feel their country's contribution to "international security", as outlined by *Securing an Open Society*, has gone too far.[161]

Conclusion

Canada's post-9/11 experience and its involvement in the U.S. led War on Terror have largely been dominated by its proximity to the United States, the world's dominant power that has come to see itself as a "society under siege." While Canadians often feel neglected and misunderstood by their southern neighbors, the attacks suddenly reminded Washington that Canada did exist; not necessarily as the U.S.' number one trading partner, a fact largely ignored by a great majority of Americans and many of their leaders, but as a potential "haven" for terrorists and, therefore, a threat to American security.

The Canada-U.S. border, the longest undefended border in the world, has repeatedly come under renewed scrutiny. For decades, Canada has often been branded by both the American political establishment and the media as a country that was "soft" — soft on communism during the Cold War and on terrorism since the late 1990s, with predictable implications for border security, trade and sovereignty. Regrettably, the unsubstantiated belief that some of the 9/11 attackers had entered the U.S. from Canada continues to re-emerge occasionally among top U.S. officials and various media outlets, the most recent example coming from the new Secretary of Homeland Security, Janet Napolitano, someone who should have been better briefed on security matters and Canada-U.S. relations.

The Bush administration's obsession with international terrorism has constituted a serious challenge to Canada's values, its sense of sovereignty and, perhaps most important of all, its vital trading partnership with the U.S. Since 2001, every Canadian government has acknowledged that reality, taking a series of bold steps to reassure their American counterparts that Canada was serious in fighting terrorism and ready to stand by its "best friend" and ally. Before the end of 2001, the Anti-Terrorist Act, also known as Bill C-36 was passed by the House of Commons, with remarkably little debate on the possible implications for civil liberties. The legislation was far-reaching as it allowed "preventive arrests," secret "investigative hearings" and added surveillance powers, all measures that, according to the Canadian Bar Association "dramatically expand state powers at the expense of due process and individual rights and freedoms."

One particular issue arose with the introduction of a new legal mechanism known as the security certificate, which initially gave the government full power to detain, interrogate and eventually deport foreign nationals or non-citizens under the suspicion of human rights violations or ties to organized crimes and terrorist organizations. In 2007, the Supreme Court of Canada ruled the whole process unconstitutional and in violation of the 1982 Canadian Charter of Rights and Freedom, prompting the Conservative government to propose some amendments. To date, six individuals remain the object of a security certificate and are under tight house arrest.

The many critics, among them the Canadian Council for Refugees and Amnesty International, have repeatedly denounced the certificate as a violation of human rights, in part because of a lack of transparency and the impossibility of appealing the decision. Complaints against the security certificate have been tied to accusations of ethnic profiling that targets Muslim Canadians and other visible minorities. "Canadians pride themselves on ideals of tolerance, inclusion and the belief that immigrants should have the same rights as Canadian citizens," commented a *Washington Post* article from December 2003. "At the same time, the country is wrestling with how to protect national security and answer critics who contend that the country's liberal immigration policies make Canada easy prey for terrorists."[162] The debate is ongoing.

Following the 9/11 attacks, security and intelligence budgets spiked dramatically and the government launched a widespread review of its immigration and refugee policies with the purpose of greater harmonization with U.S. practices. Such frenzy inevitably led to abuses, the most notorious of all being the case of Canadian citizen Maher Arar. The RCMP passed information to U.S. officials, leading to his arrest at JFK airport and a forcibly deported to his native Syria, where he was tortured.

Then there is the refusal of the Conservative government to seek the extradition and repatriation of Omar Khadr, a Canadian citizen charged with war crimes for supporting terrorism in Afghanistan and held at the U.S. base of Guantanamo Bay. The government is holding firm despite a recent ruling of the Federal Court of Canada.

Perhaps the most controversial human rights issue has been the question of the insurgents taken prisoner by the Canadian Forces in Afghanistan. Of note, they are called "detainees," not prisoners of war, a convenient use of semantics to deny them elementary rights under the Geneva Conventions. As Ottawa has consistently refused to consider establishing detention camps in Afghanistan, the prisoners have been transferred to American custody. Many, like Khadr, ended up at Guantanamo Bay, where they were submitted to cruel interrogation techniques, or so Amnesty International and other human rights organizations have contended.

The issue got the attention of the media and grew into a full political crisis in the spring of 2007, when the Military Police Complaints Commission, an independent civilian agency set up to examine complaints pertaining to the conduct of military police members, came to investigate the alleged abuse of three detainees by the Canadian Forces before their transfer to the Afghan police. The government acted quickly to put the matter to rest and negotiated an agreement with Kabul, granting Canadian government representatives in Afghanistan full access to detainees after their transfer and regular notifications as to their location and well-being. The Afghan government also agreed not to transfer detainees handed over by Canada to another power (meaning the U.S., of course) without permission to do so.

Overall, the many problems that arose from various new anti-terrorist laws, together with Canada's increased military commitment in Afghanistan, have come to challenge the country's traditional approaches towards immigration, human rights and peacekeeping. Although Canada declined to join the U.S.-led coalition in Iraq, its involvement in Afghanistan has gradually deepened. The fundamental problem with that involvement was summarized aptly by Wesley Wark, a professor of international relations at the University of Toronto: "The government showed little inclination to engage in a strategic analysis of the new security environment. We went to war without deciding what kind of war it was."[163]

In many ways, this absence of strategic analysis demonstrates that Canada's response to the attacks on 9/11 has been primarily a *reaction to* Washington's reaction. Considering how dependent Canada has become economically and on matters of continental security, Ottawa had little choice but to emphasize on numerous occasions it was determined to play its part in the global War on Terror. Too much was at stake. Jean Chrétien attempted to distance his government from the Bush's administration War on Terror, yet the extraordinary measures that were implemented under his tenure, followed by Paul Martin's national security strategy, a first in Canadian history, have largely achieved their initial goals: to fight global terrorism through a "made in Canada" approach and to maintain the necessary level of good relations with Washington while preserving Canadian sovereignty from too many infringements. This is a fragile compromise, no doubt.

And yes, as Wesley Wark also pointed out, behind the rhetoric of Paul Martin's foreword to his *"Securing an Open Society,"* "the National Security Policy contains little in the way of reference to human right protections or advocacy. The emphasis in the document is on 'securing'; the 'open society' is more or less taken for granted. Paradoxically, unlike a strategy statement fixated on terrorist threats and responses, an 'all hazards' approach, so much in tune with Canadian experience and outlook, may have reduced the visibility of human rights concerns."[164] There have been abuses. But, in the climate of suspicion and paranoia that blew our way from Washington under George W. Bush, preserving Canada's independence and freedom of action came at a price.

Canada's War on Terror — assuming we can call it that — has remained purposely vague, with governments attempting to artfully balance the need for increased security, the need to maintain human rights and the political compulsion to integrate policies with those of our neighbor and traditional ally, the United States. Overall, under the circumstances and despite the heavy cost paid thus far in Afghanistan, those governments have largely been successful. The "Canadian way" has been somewhat preserved.

Notes

1 Prime Minister Jean Chrétien, *The Globe and Mail*, September 11, 2001.

2 Jean-Marie Colombani, "We Are All Americans," article, *Le Monde*, September 12, 2001.

3 Colin Powell, "Perspectives: Powell Defends a First Strike as Iraq Option," interview, *New York Times*, September 8, 2002, p. 18.

4 "The National Security Strategy of the United States of America September 2002, p.14. Available online at http://www.whitehouse.gov/nsc/nss.pdf.

5 Quoted in Mark Burgess, "A Brief History of Terrorism," Center For Defense Information. Available online at http://www.cdi.org/friendlyversion/printversion.cfm?documentID=1502. September 9, 2008.

6 Max Weber, "Politics as a Vocation", lecture given at the University of Munich in January 1919. Available online at http://www.ne.jp/asahi/moriyuki/abukuma/weber/lecture/politics_vocation.html. September 9, 2008.

7 Barbara W. Tuchman, *The Proud Tower, A Portrait of The World Before The War*, Ballantine Books, New York, p. 99.

8 Osama Bin Laden alleged post-9/11 quotes, reported by the *Washington Times*, November 2001.

9 Department of Defense, Dictionary of Military and Associated Terms, 12 April 2008 (As Amended through 26 August 2008); p. 152. Available online at http://www.dtic.mil/doctrine/jel/new_pubs/jp1_02.pdf. October 5, 2008.

10 Ibid, p. 40.

11 G.W. Bush, *Address to a Joint Session of Congress and the American People*, Washington DC, 20 September 2001.

12 Donald Rumsfeld, Press Conference, NATO HQ, Brussels, 6 June 2002.

13 President Bill Clinton, presidential address, August 20, 1998. Accessible at http://www.pbs.org/newshour/bb/military/july-dec98/clinton2_8-20.html

14 Website Alliance of Civilizations – Introduction. http://www.unaoc.org/content/view/86/122/lang,english/

15 G.W. Bush, *Address to a Joint Session of Congress and the American People*, Washington DC, 20 September 2001.

16 G.W. Bush, *Address to the nation*, September 16, 2001.

17 Ronald Reagan, Remarks at the Opening of the "American Cowboy" exhibit at the Library of Congress, 24 March 1983

Available on line at: http://west.stanford.edu/cgi-bin/pager.php?id=10

18 George Washington, First inaugural address, April 30, 1789. The Avalon Project. http://avalon.law.yale.edu/18th_century/wash1.asp

19 George W. Bush, "Overview of America's International Strategy," West Point, New York, June 1, 2002. In Crosscurrents, International Relations, Fourth Edition. Edited by Mark Charlton, Trinity Western University, p.99.

20 British Release Evidence Against bin Laden, quoted in Mary Ellen O'Connell "The Myth of Pre-emptive Self-Defense, August 2002. http://www.asil.org/taskforce/oconnell.pdf (last visited November 15, 2008).

21 http://www.whitehouse.gov/news/releases/2002/01/20020129-11.html

22 George W. Bush, "The National Security Strategy of the United States of America," September 17, 2002. In Crosscurrents, International Relations, Fourth Edition. Edited by Mark Charlton, Trinity Western University, p.97.

23 Alan M. Dershowitz, *Preemption, a Knife that Cuts Both Ways*, W.W. Norton & Company, 2006.

24 "The National Security Strategy of the United States of America," September 2002, accessible at http://www.whitehousegov/nsc/nss.pdf

25 George W. Bush, "Overview of America's International Strategy," West Point, New York, June 1, 2002. In Crosscurrents, International Relations, Fourth Edition. Edited by Mark Charlton, Trinity Western University, p.99.

26 Donald Rumsfeld, Press Conference, NATO HQ, Brussels, 6 June 2002.

27 UN Charter, article 2, paragraph 4.

28 *The National Security of the United States of America*, September 2002, p.15. http://www.globalsecurity.org/military/library/policy/national/nss-020920.pdf

29 Security Council Resolution 487, June 19, 1981.

30 "The Current Regulation of the Use of Force," edited by A. Cassese, Martinus Nijhoff Publishers, 1986, p. 522.

31 Anthony D'Amato, *Israel's Air Strike Against The Osiraq Reactor: A Retrospective*, Temple International and Comparative Law Journal 259 (1996). Accessible at http://anthonydamato.law.northwestern.edu/Adobefiles/A961-Isr.pdf

32 Paul W. Schroeder, "Iraq, the Case Against Preemptive War," *The American Conservative*, October 21, 2002, p. 7.

33 David F. Burg and L. Edward Purcell, Almanac of World War I, University Press of Kentucky, 2004, p.522.

34 Winston Churchill, *The Gathering Storm*, Boston, Houghton Mifflin, 1948, pp. 15-16.

35 Steven R. Prebeck, *Preventive attacks in the 1990s*, 1993. Abstract. Accessible at http://www.scribd.com/doc/1434299/US-Air-Force-prebeck

36 Powell, Secretary Colin L. (February 5, 2003). "Remarks to the United Nations Security Council". New York City: U.S. Department of State. Accessible at http://www.state.gov/secretary/former/powell/remarks/2003/17300.htm

37 Kerr, R.J., *et al.* (29 July 2004) "Intelligence and Analysis on Iraq: Issues for the Intelligence Community," MORI Doc. ID 1245667 (Langley, VA: Central Intelligence Agency)

38 US Department of Defense (June 2008): Measuring Security and Stability in Iraq

39 Quote by Reuters on 7 March 2002, in Fraser Cameron, *US Foreign Policy After The Cold War, Global Hegemon or Reluctant Sheriff?* Routledge, New York, 2004, p. 194.

40 Speech by Dominique de Villepin, Foreign Affairs Minister to the United Nations Security Council, 19 March 2003. Accessible at http://www.ambafrance-uk.org/article.php3?id_article=4917

41 Statement on Iraq by eight European leaders, January 30, 2003; accessible at http://www.acronym.org.uk/docs/0301/doc25.htm

42 Neta Crawford, "The Slippery Slope to Preventive War." In Crosscurrents, International Relations, Fourth Edition. Edited by Mark Charlton, Trinity Western University, p. 115.

43 Prime Minister Jean Chrétien, *The Globe and Mail*, September 11, 2001.

44 General Abizaid, testimony before the US Senate Armed Services Committee, May 19, 2004. *Final Report of the Independent Panel to review DoD Detention Operations*, August 2004.

45 The White House, *National Strategy for Combating Terrorism*, page 2. Accessible at http://www.state.gov/documents/organization/60172.pdf

46 http://www.whitehouse.gov/news/releases/2001/09/20010914-4.html

47 http://www.whitehouse.gov/news/releases/2006/03/20060309-4.html

48 Karen Gullo, "Government Investigation Focuses on bin Laden; Police Check Whether Hijackers Entered from Canada," Associated Press, September 13, 2001. http://archive.southcoasttoday.com/daily/09-01/09-13-01/a02wn026.htm

49 Richard A. Clarke, *Against All Enemies, Inside America's War on Terror*, Free Press, New York, 2004, p. 238.

50 United States Congressional Record (Senate), October 25, 2001, S10990-S1060, accessible at http://www.fas.org/sgp/congress/2001/s102501.html

51 Stewart Bell, *Cold Terror: How Canada Nurtures and Exports Terrorism Around the World*, Toronto: John Wiley & Sons, 2004.

52 See, for instance, Diane Francis, *Immigration: The Economic Case*, Toronto: Key Porter Books, 2002; Daniel Stoffmann, *Who Gets In: What's Wrong With Canada's Immigration Program — And How To Fix It*, Toronto: Macfarlane Walter and Ross, 2002; Charles Campbell, *Betrayal and Deceit: The Politics of Canadian Immigration*, Vancouver: Jasmine Books, 2000).

53 The Canadian Institute, *One Issue, Two Voices: Threat Perceptions in the United States and Canada*, Washington DC: Woodrow Wilson Center for Scholars, 2005, p. 10-19.

54 Michael Ignatieff, "Time to Walk the Walk," *National Post*, February 14, 2003.

55 Ward Elcock, "Countering the Terrorist Threat," Speech, Vancouver Board of Trade, November 7, 2002.

56 Canadian Security Intelligence Service (CSIS), *International Terrorism: The Threat to Canada,* report no 2000/04, May 3, 2000. http://www.csis.gc.ca/pblctns/prspctvs/200004-eng.asp (accessed on January 17, 2009).

57 CSIS, *2000 Public Report,* June 2001.

58 Allan R. Gregg, "Scary New World," *Maclean's*, December 31, 2001.

59 Arne Kislenko, "Guarding the Border: The Dilemmas and Realities of Law Enforcement in Canada's Immigration System," p. 7.

60 Bill C-11, Summary, accessible at http://www2.parl.gc.ca/HousePublications/Publication.aspx?DocId=2330877&Language=e&Mode=1

61 Canada Border Services Agency, website accessible at http://www.cbsa-asfc.gc.ca/agency-agence/stca-etps-eng.html

62 Federal Court of Canada, website, accessible at http://decisions.fct-cf.gc.ca/en/2007/2007fc1262/2007fc1262.html

63 Ronald Kessler, *The CIA At War: Inside the Secret Campaign Against Terror*, New York, St Martin's Press, 2003, p. 277.

64 Dana Priest, "Deported Terror Suspect Details Torture in Syria. Canadian's Case Called Typical of CIA," *Washington Post*, November 5, 2003.

65 Michael Den Tandt, "Deportation Pact Useless, Inquiry Told," *Globe and Mail*, June 8, 2005.

66 "'Come clean' on Arar, Harper asks U.S.," CBC, October 5, 2006.

67 Allan Gotlieb, "A Grand Bargain with the US," *National Post*, March 5, 2003.

68 *Toronto Star*, "Clinton's smart power," January 14, 2009.

69 *Globe and Mail*, September 21, 2001.

70 *Toronto Sun*, September 21, 2001.

71 Christie Blatchford, "Canada does not rate a mention," *National Post*, September 21, 2001.

72 *Globe and Mail*, "Ridge, Manley sign 'smart border' declaration," December 12, 2001.

73 Prime Minister of Canada, "Security and Prosperity Partnership of North America," news release, March 23, 2005.

74 *Canada committed to Afghan mission, Harper tells troops*, CBC news website, 13 March 2006. Last updated 13 March 2006. Accessed 28 June 2008. URL: http://www.cbc.ca/story/world/national/2006/03/13/harper_afghanistan060313.html

75 Jennifer Welsh, *At Home in the World, Canada's Global Vision for the 21st Century*, Harper Collins, Toronto, 2004, p. 11.

76 Tad Szulc, "Don't Take Canada For Granted." *Parade Magazine*. February 20, 1994.

77 Reg Whitaker, "More or Less Than Meets the Eye? The New National Security Agenda," in G. Bruce Doern, ed., *How Ottawa Spends, 2003-2004: Regime Change and Policy Shift*, Oxford University Press, Toronto, 2003, p. 45.

78 Bill C-36, accessible at http://www2.parl.gc.ca/HousePublications/Publication.aspx?DocId=2330951&Language=e&Mode=1

79 *Globe and Mail*, Shawn McCarthy, "Pulled Ever Deeper into US Orbit," January 8, 2002.

80 "Oral Question Period," Stockwell Day, Leader of the Official Opposition. In Canada, House of Commons Legislative Debates, 37th Parliament, 1st Session, edited Hansard, number 79, Monday, September 17, 2001. http://www2.parl.gc.ca/HousePublications/Publication.aspx?Language=E&Mode=1&Parl=37&Ses=1&DocId=653212

81 Cabinet notes, May 15, 1968, Press Release, May 29, 1968, Office of the Prime Minister Office, quoted in J.L. Granatstein, Canada's Army, Waging War and Keeping The Peace, University of Toronto Press, Toronto, 2002, p. 361.

82 Office of the Prime Minister, Press Release, May 29, 1968; in J.L. Granatstein, *Canada's Army, Waging War and Keeping The Peace*, University of Toronto Press, 2002, p. 361.

83 Confidential source, cited in J.L. Granatstein & Robert Bothwell, *Pirouette, Pierre Trudeau and Canadian Foreign Policy*, University of Toronto Press, 1990, p. 239.

84 Sean Maloney, *War without Battles: Canada's NATO Brigade in Germany, 1951-1993*, McGraw-Hill Ryerson Trade, Toronto, 1997, p. 242-3.

85 J.L.Granatstein, *Canada's Army, Waging War and Keeping The Peace*, p. 391.

86 Ibid. p. 393.

87 Francis Fukuyama, *The End of History and The Last Man*, Penguin 1992.

88 Foreign Affairs and International Trade Canada, website, *Canada and the World*, Summary; accessible at http://www.dfait-maeci.gc.ca/foreign_policy/cnd-world/summary-en.asp

89 Remarks by David Kilgour, University of Alberta international week, 2004, "Canada Peacekeeping Role, then and Now." Accessible at http://www.david-kilgour.com/mp/Peacekeeping%20U%20of%20A.htm

90 Douglas Rand, ed. *Canada's National Defense, Volume 1, Defense Policy*, McGill — Queen University Press, 1999, p. 293.

91 Defense White Paper, Ottawa, 1994, p. 2.

92 Department of Foreign Affairs and International Trade, "Canada and Peacekeeping," January 1995, pp. 1-3

93 J.L. Granatstein, Canada's Army, p. 419

94 Ibid. p. 406.

95 The Somalia commission's conclusions, under the title *Dishonoured Legacy* are available on CD-ROM: *Information Legacy: A Compendium of Source Material from the Commission of Inquiry into the Deployment of Canadian Forces to Somalia* (Ottawa, 1997).

96 Stacey, *The Military Problems of Canada*, pp. 29-35.

97 National Archives of Canada. Mackenzie King Diary, 20, 23 and 24 April 1940.

98 Ronald Reagan, national televised address, March 23, 1983. Accessible at http://www.fas.org/spp/starwars/offdocs/rrspch.htm

99 *1994 White Paper*, p. 23.

100 Janice Gross Stein and Eugene Lang, The Unexpected War, Canada in Kandahar, Penguin Canada, 2007, p. 20.

101 Janice Gross Stein and Eugene Lang, The Unexpected War, pp. 47-48.

102 *National Post*, Chris Wattie, "Forces' Last Chance to Show Country What They Can do," January 10, 2003.

103 Canada, House of Commons, Legislative Debates. 37th Parliament, 2nd Session, John McCallum, "Oral Question Period," February 12, 2003. Available online at http://www2.parl.gc.ca/HousePublications/Publication.aspx?Language=E&Mode=1&Parl=37&Ses=2&DocId=695956

104 Julian Beltrame, "Canada to Stay Out of Iraq War," Maclean's Magazine, 31 March 2003.
http://www.thecanadianencyclopedia.com/index.cfm?PgNm=TCE&Params=M1ARTM0012457

105 Jean Chrétien, *My Years As Prime Minister*, Vintage Canada Edition, 2008, p. 313.

106 Tim Harper, *The Toronto Star*, www.thestar.com, Canadians Back Chrétien on War, Poll finds, 22 March 2003.
http://25461.vws.magma.ca/admin/articles/torstar-24-03-2003c.html

107 Quoted on CTV.ca, "Americans 'disappointed' with Canada: Cellucci", 25 March 2003.

http://www.ctv.ca/servlet/ArticleNews/story/CTVNews/1048603041834_119

108 Quoted in the *Globe and Mail*, Michael Den Tandt, "Energy-hogging U.S. can't stay sore at us forever, 3 April 2003.

109 CTV.ca, "Americans 'disappointed' with Canada: Cellucci," op. cit.

110 Jean Chrétien, *My Years as Prime Minister*, p. 319.

111 Public Safety Canada, Executive Summary, *Securing an Open Society: Canada's National Security Policy*. Last updated 25 September 2007. publicsafety.gc.ca. URL: http://www.publicsafety.gc.ca/pol/ns/secpol04-eng.aspx

112 *Securing an Open Society: Canada's National Security Policy*, Canada National Library of Canada. Privy Council Office. Introduction by Paul Martin. ISBN 0-662-36982-3 Cat. No. CP22-77/2004E-PDF.
URL: http://www.bcp-pco.gc.ca/docs/information/Publications/natsec-secnat/natsec-secnat_e.pdf

113 The *Globe and Mail*, Wesley Wark, "Martin's New Security Agenda, Feeling Safe Yet?" 18 December 2003.

114 Reg Whitaker, "Made in Canada? The New Public Safety Paradigm, in *How Canada Spends, 2005-2006*, edited by Bruce Doern, McGill-Queen's Press, pp. 90-2.

115 Ibid. p. 77

116 Barry Cooper, "Martin's Cabinet Picked for PR," *Saskatoon Star-Phoenix*, 22 December 2003.

117 Public Safety Canada, Executive Summary, op. cit.

118 Department of Public Safety and Emergency Preparedness, "About Us" http://www.psepcsppcc.gc.ca/abt/index-en.asp

119 Public Safety Canada, website, Government Operations Centre, http://www.publicsafety.gc.ca/prg/em/goc/index-eng.aspx

120 Office of the Auditor General, 12 February 2005. www.canada.gc.ca

121 Jennifer Welsh, At Home In The World, Canada's Global Vision For The 21st Century, HarperCollins Publishers, Toronto, 2004. p. 121.

122 Office of the Auditor General, "National Security in Canada — the 2001 Anti-Terrorism Initiative," March 2004. http://www.oag-bvg.gc.ca/internet/English/osm_20040330_e_21703.html

123 Senate Standing Committee on National Security and Defense, 6 December 2004, Canadian Security Guidebook, An Update of Security Problems in Search of Solutions. 2005 edition.

124 37th Parliament, 3rd Session. Parliament of Canada. 27 April 2004. www.parl.gc.ca

125 CTV news, 27 April 2004, CTV.ca

126 The Globe and Mail, Barrie McKenna, "U.S. Praises Security Blueprint," 26 April 2004

127 The White House, "President Discusses Strong Relationship with Canada," Halifax, Nova Scotia, 1 December 2004. URL: http://www.whitehouse.gov/news/releases/2004/12/20041201-4.html

128 Ibid, p. vii.

129 Speaking notes for the Honorable Ann McLellan, Securing an open society: building a national security policy for Canada, April 27, 2004. Public Safety Canada. Publicsafety.gc.ca. Last updated 19 December 2007. Accessed 28 June 2008. URL: http://www.publicsafety.gc.ca/media/sp/2004/sp20040407-eng.aspx

130 The Toronto Star, Ben Rowswell, "McLellan's U.S. Challenge," 18 December 2003

131 Peter Andreas, "A Tale of Two Borders: The U.S.-Mexico and U.S.-Canada Lines After 9-11," Brown University, p.1. URL: http://www.ccis-ucsd.org/publications/wrkg77.pdf

132 The Toronto Sun, Greg Weston, "Fix Leaky Borders: U.S." 20 September 2001

133 Public Safety and Emergency Preparedness Canada, "Securing an Open Society: Canada's National Security Policy." Government of Canada, 2004. URL: www.canada.gc.ca

134 The Globe and Mail, Paul Koring, "Bush adds $2 billion to border pot," 26 January 2002

135 Graham Flack, quoted in Jennifer Welsh, At Home In The World, op. cit., p.59.

136 Government of Canada, "Securing an Open Society, Canada's National Security Policy," URL: http://www.pco-bcp.gc.ca/docs/information/Publications/natsec-secnat/natsec-secnat-eng.pdf

137 Anne McLellan, Canada's Deputy Prime Minister and Minister of Public Safety and Emergency Preparedness, March 25, 2004. http://www.canadianembassy.org/defense/quotes-en.asp

138 Royal Canadian Mounted Police website, Integrated Border Enforcement Team program (IBETs), 2006 Joint Cross-Border Operations. Last updated 28 April 2008. Accessed 28 June 2008. URL: http://www.rcmp-grc.gc.ca/security/ibets_success_e.htm

139 Government of Canada, "Securing an Open Society, Canada's National Security Policy," p.11. URL: http://www.pco-bcp.gc.ca/docs/information/Publications/natsec-secnat/natsec-secnat-eng.pdf

140 Reg Whitaker, "Made in Canada? The New Public Safety Paradigm," in How Canada Spends 2005-2006, op. cit., p.85.

141 R. James Woolsey & Rachel K. Belton, "We Must Face a Connected World's 'Butterfly Effect'," Los Angeles Times, 5 May 2004. http://articles.latimes.com/2004/may/05/opinion/oe-woolsey5?pg=1

142 "Smallpox fiasco," editorial, Washington Post, July 14, 2003. http://www.ph.ucla.edu/epi/Bioter/spoxfiasco.html

143 Health Canada, Canada's health care system, http://www.hc-sc.gc.ca/hcs-sss/medi-assur/index-eng.php

144 Public Health Agency of Canada, website, http://www.phac-aspc.gc.ca/media/nr-rp/2009/2009_0507_h1n1-eng.php

145 Report of the Standing Committee on Foreign Affairs and International Trade, Partners in North America: Advancing Canada's Relations with the United States and Mexico, December 2002.

146 For an extensive account on the post Cold War era before 9/11, see Mitchell Reiss and Robert S. Litwak (eds.) Nuclear Proliferation After the Cold War, Washington, D.C.: Woodrow Wilson Center Press and Johns Hopkins University Press, 1994.

147 National Defense and the Canadian Armed Forces, www.forces.gc.ca, Canada and Ballistic Missile Defense http://www.forces.gc.ca/site/news-nouvelles/view-news-afficher-nouvelles-eng.asp?id=1064

148 Cole Harvey, "GAO Criticizes Missile Defense Programs", Arms Control Association, April 2009
http://www.armscontrol.org/act/2009_04/GAOmissileDefense

149 David Pratt to Donald Rumsfeld, 8 July 2007, in Janice Gross Stein and Eugene Lang, The Unexpected War, p. 126.

150 The Globe and Mail, "Excerpt from Bush Speech", December 2, 2004.

151 The Toronto Star, Chantal Hebert, "Missile Defense PM's Major Irritant," February 4, 2005.

152 General Hillier's first speech as Chief of Defense Staff, February 5, 2005, Dept. of National Defense, CTV.ca archives, The Canadian Press.
http://www.ctv.ca/servlet/ArticleNews/story/CTVNews/20080415/hillier_in_brief_080415/20080415?hub=Specials

153 Government of Canada, Canada's International Policy Statement — A Role of Pride and Influence in the World-DEFENSE-Summary. Ottawa, Department of National Defense, 2005, p.3.

154 "Why We Are There", National Defense and the Canadian Forces, 5 January 2007, www.forces.gc.ca/site/newsroom/view_news_e.asp?id-1703

155 Interview with Paul Martin, February 7, 2007, quoted in Janice Gross Stein and Eugene Lang, The Unexpected War, Canada in Kandahar, Penguin Canada, 2007, p. 189.

156 CTV.ca: "A dangerous mission for Canadian troops," April 10, 2006.
http://www.ctv.ca/servlet/ArticleNews/story/CTVNews/20050804_afghanistan_timeline_050804

157 CTV.ca: "Operation Medusa, a "significant" success: NATO. September 17, 2006.
http://www.ctv.ca/servlet/ArticleNews/story/CTVNews/20060917/suicide_bomb_060917?s_name=&no_ads=

158 Angus Reid Global Monitor. Polls and research. "Support for Afghanistan Role Drops in Canada." August 6, 2006. http://www.angus-reid.com/polls/view/12756

159 CBCnews.ca, "Canada in Afghanistan", February 10, 2009.
http://www.cbc.ca/canada/story/2009/02/10/f-afghanistan.html

160 The Globe and Mail, Steven Chase, "U.S. declines to press Canada on Afghanistan," 11 February 2009.
http://www.theglobeandmail.com/servlet/story/RTGAM.20090211.wobamamilitary11/BNStory/Afghanistan/home

161 CBCnews.ca. Public support for Afghan mission lowest ever: Poll. September 5, 2008. http://www.cbc.ca/canada/story/2008/09/05/poll-afghan.html

162 DeNeen L. Brown, "Canadians' Culture of Tolerance Is Tested by Cases Against Arabs," Washington Post, December 17, 2003.

163 Wesley Wark, "Canada and the 'War on Terror'", in Ideas&s, volume 2, 2005, p.19.

164 Wesley Wark, "National Security and Human Rights Concerns in Canada: A Survey of Eight Critical Issues in the Post-9/11 Environment," Canadian Human Rights Commission, 2006. p. 8.

Selected Secondary Sources

Globe and Mail
Le Monde
Los Angeles Times
National Post
New York Times
Toronto Stat
Toronto Sun
Saskatoon – Star Phoenix
Washington Post
Washington Times
Associated Press
CBCNews
CTV.ca

Bell, Stewart. *Cold Terror: How Canada Nurtures and Exports Terrorism Around the World*, Toronto: John Wiley & Sons, 2004

Campbell, Charles. *Betrayal and Deceit: The Politics of Canadian Immigration*, Vancouver: Jasmine Books, 2000

Charlton, Mark ed. *Crosscurrents, International Relations, Fourth Edition.* Trinity Western University, 2006

Chrétien, Jean. *My Years As Prime Minister*, Vintage Canada Edition, 2008

Churchill,Winston. *The Gathering Storm*, Boston, Houghton Mifflin, 1948

Clarke, Richard A. *Against All Enemies, Inside America's War on Terror*, Free Press, New York, 2004,

Dershowitz, Alan M. *Preemption, a Knife that Cuts Both Ways*, W.W. Norton & Company, 2006

Doem, G. Bruce, ed. *How Ottawa Spends, 2003-2004: Regime Change and Policy Shift*, Oxford University Press, Toronto, 2003

Francis, Diane. *Immigration: The Economic Case*, Toronto: Key Porter Books, 2002

Fukuyama, Francis. *The End of History and The Last Man*, Penguin 1992

Granatstein, J.L. *Canada's Army, Waging War and Keeping The Peace*, University of Toronto Press, 2002

Granatstein, J.L. & Bothwell, Robert. *Pirouette, Pierre Trudeau and Canadian Foreign Policy*, University of Toronto Press, 1990

Kessler, Ronald. *The CIA At War: Inside the Secret Campaign Against Terror*, New York, St Martin's Press, 2003

Maloney, Sean. *War without Battles: Canada's NATO Brigade in Germany, 1951-1993*, McGraw-Hill Ryerson Trade, Toronto, 1997

Prebeck, Steven R. *Preventive attacks in the 1990s*, 1993.

Rand, Douglas ed. *Canada's National Defence, Volume 1, Defence Policy*, McGill – Queen University Press, 1999

Stacey, Charles. *The Military Problems of Canada*, The Ryerson Press, Toronto, 1940

Tuchman, Barbara W. *The Proud Tower, A Portrait of The World Before The War*, Ballantine Books, New York, 1996

Gross Stein, Janice and Lang, Eugene. *The Unexpected War, Canada in Kandahar*, Penguin Canada, 2007

Stoffmann, Daniel. *Who Gets In: What's Wrong With Canada's Immigration Program – And How To Fix It*, Toronto: Macfarlane Walter and Ross, 2002

Welsh, Jennifer. *At Home in the World, Canada's Global Vision for the 21st Century*, Harper Collins, Toronto, 2004

Index

A

Abizaid, General John, 38
Afghanistan, 6, 9, 11, 18-19, 38, 45, 55-57, 63, 71, 77-79, 85, 106-113, 118-120, 133
al-Qaeda, 8, 11, 18, 36, 43-44, 48, 76
American Enterprise Institute, 44
American exceptionalism, 16
Amnesty International, 117, 118
Annan, Kofi, 10
Anti-terrorism, 6
Anti-Terrorism Act, 7, 57
Arar, Maher, 37, 39, 46, 48-50, 117
Automotive Products Trade Agreement, 66
Axworthy, Lloyd, 62

B

ballistic missile defense, 74, 102, 104
Baril, General Maurice, 71
Belgium, 26
Bell, Stewart, 43, 125
Bethmann- Hollweg, Theobald von, 26
Bin Laden, Osama, 4, 121
Blix, Hans, 80
BMD, 2, 74, 75, 100-106
Bush Administration, 6, 8
Bush Doctrine, 12, 20-21, 26, 92
Bush, George. See Bush, George W.. See Bush, George W.. See Bush, George W.

Bush, George H. W., 22
Bush. George W., 8, 13-15, 19, 31, 35, 38, 40, 49, 52, 55, 70, 82, 102, 104-105, 120, 122-123

C

Canada in the World, 67
Canada's Coastlines, 89
Canadian Airborne Regiment, 70
Canadian Bar Association, 116
Canadian Charter of Rights and Freedom, 116
Canadian Council for Refugees, 117
Canadian Forces, 70-71, 75, 77, 79, 85-86, 107, 109, 111, 118, 128, 132
Canadian Security Intelligence Service, 44, 125
Caplan, Elinor, 41
Celluci, Paul, 72
Cheney, Dick, 22
Chrétien, Jean, 1, 35, 52, 58, 69, 79, 80, 119, 121, 124, 128
Churchill, Winston, 26, 123
CIDA. See International Development Agency
Clarke, Richard, 42
Clinton, Bill, 9, 52, 74, 97, 122
Clinton, Hillary, 51
Cold War, 20, 22, 67, 68, 101, 107, 115, 132
Commission of Inquiry into the Deployment of Canadian forces to Somalia, 71
Congress, U. S., 3, 8, 14, 36, 38-40, 53, 57, 102, 122
continental security, 53, 59, 74, 78, 88, 119
counter-terrorism, 6, 39
Crawford, Neta, 33, 124
CSIS. *See* Canadian Security Intelligence Service
CTV News, 91
Cuban missile crisis, 65
Customs and Immigration. *See* U.S. Customs and Immigration
Cyprus, 66
Czechoslovakia, 64

D

D'Amato, Anthony, 24, 123

Darfur, the, 110
Defense Policy Guidance, 22
Defense, Department of, 31, 65, 71, 110, 121, 124
Defense, Permanent Joint Board on, 73
Department of Foreign Affairs and International Trade, 128
Dershowitz, Alan, 20
Diefenbaker, John, 73
Dorgan, Byron, 42

E

Eggleton, Art, 77
Eisenhower, Dwight, 15
EKOS Research Associates, 44, 81
European Union, 1, 33

F

FAST. See Free and Secure Trade. See Free and Secure Trade
Federal Court, 48, 50, 118, 126
Foreign Affairs and International Trade, Department of, 67
Fox. Vincente, 55
France, 26, 27, 80
Fraser, Brig.-Gen. David, 111
Fraser, Sheila, 88
Free and Secure Trade, 94

G

Gandhi, Indira, 4
Germany, Nazi, 13, 26-27
globalization, 11
GOC. *See* Government Operation Centre
Government Operation Centre, 87
Graham, Bill, 85, 106
Granastein, J.L., 66
Granatstein, J.L., 70, 127
Great Britain, 27
Guantanamo Bay, 6, 37, 50, 118

H

Haiti, 68
Hamas, 11
Harper, Stephen, 49, 56, 84, 110, 112-113
Hébert, Chantal, 105
Hezbollah, 11
Hillier, General Rick, 106
Hiroshima, 13
Hitler, 27
Homeland Security, Department of, 6, 41, 87, 91
House of Commons Foreign Affairs Committee, 100
Huntington, Samuel, 10
Hussein, Saddam, 10, 19, 29, 31, 33, 79, 80

I

IBETS. See Integrated Border Enforcement Team program
Ignatieff, Michael, 44, 125
Integrated Border Enforcement Team program, 96, 131
International Convention for the Suppression of Financing of Terrorism, 57
International Development Agency, 108
Iran, 19, 31, 32, 74, 102
Iraq, 5, 6, 9, 19, 22-23, 25, 29-34, 36, 55, 58, 78-80, 82, 86, 97, 102, 106, 109, 113, 119, 121, 123-124, 128
Israel, 5, 11, 23-25, 31, 123
Israeli-Palestinian conflict, 5

J

Japan, 12-13, 28, 29
Jihad, 14
Johnson, Lyndon, 66
Joint Task Force 2, 62, 77

K

Kandahar, 56, 76-77, 108-109, 111, 132, 136
Kenny, Colin, 89
Kergin, Michael, 80

King, William Lyon Mackenzie, 72
Kislenko, Arne, 2, 47, 125
Kuwait, 31

L

La Presse, 81
Le Monde, 1, 121, 134
Libby, Lewis, 22
Liberation Tigers of Tamil Eelam, 43
Libya, 9
London, Treaty of, 26

M

Mandela, Nelson, 3
Manifest Destiny, 15
Manley, John, 60, 112
Martin, Paul, 49, 55, 83, 85-86, 91, 95, 100, 103-104, 106, 109-110, 119, 120, 129, 132
McCallum, John, 77, 128
McLean's, 80
McLellan, Ann, 86, 92, 130
Mexico, 51, 54, 92, 93-94, 130-131
Middle East, 11, 29, 32, 45, 65
Midway, Battle of, 28
Military Police Complaints Commission, 118
Mulroney, Brian, 52, 69
Munich agreement, 26, 27
Munich Olympic Games, 9
Myers, General Richard, 78

N

NAFTA, 51
Nagasaki, 13
Napolitano, Janet, 1, 115
National Post, 54, 79, 125-126, 128, 134
National Security in Canada — the 2001 Anti-Terrorism initiative, 88
National Security Strategy of the United States of America, 20, 23, 92, 121-123

NATO. *See* North Atlantic Treaty Organization
NEXUS program, 93
NORAD. See North American Air Agreement
North American Aerospace Defense Command, 74
North American Air Agreement, 74
North Atlantic Treaty Organization, 17
North Korea, 18, 28, 74, 102
nuclear deterrence, 65

O

Obama, Barack, 36, 50, 113
Operation Enduring Freedom, 18, 38, 77, 108
Operation Medusa, 111, 132
Osirak, 24
Ottoman Empire, 30

P

Parti Quebecois, 81
Patriot Act, 6, 40, 48, 57, 61
peacekeeping, 63- 66, 68, 69- 71, 76, 107, 109-110, 119
Pearl Harbor, 12-13, 28
Pearson. Lester, 63
Pentagon, 1, 4, 8, 12, 53, 57
Phelan, Justice Michael, 48
Powell, Colin, 1, 29, 53, 93, 121
Pratt, David, 86, 103
Prebeck, Steven, 27
protectionism, 51
Provincial Reconstruction Team, 108
PRT. See Provincial Reconstruction Team

R

RCMP. See Royal Canadian Mounted Police
Reagan, Ronald, 9, 14-15, 74
Refugee and Immigration Protection Act, 47
Ressam, Ahmed, 42
Rice, Condoleeza, 70

Robertson, George, 76
Roosevelt, Franklin, 12, 72-73
Royal Canadian Mounted Police, 61, 131
Rumsfeld, Donald, 9, 22, 76, 78, 103, 122-123
Rwanda, 68

S

Safe Third Country Agreement, 47-48, 95
SARS. *See* Severe Acute Respiratory Syndrome
Saudi Arabia, 31, 42
Schroeder, Paul W., 25, 123
Securing an Open Society: Canada's National Security Policy, 83
Security and Prosperity Partnership, 55, 126
security certificate, 116-117
self-defense, 17-18, 20, 22-23
Senate Standing Committee on National Security and Defense, 89, 130
Severe Acute Respiratory Syndrome, 45
Smart Border, 54-55, 92-94, 96
Snow, John, 91
Somalia, 70, 75, 128
Soviet Union, 15, 20-21, 27, 32, 64-67, 93, 101
Stockwell Day, 62
Strategic Defense Initiative, 74
Sudan, 9
Supreme Court of Canada, 116

T

Taliban, 18, 19, 38, 78, 108, 109, 110, 111
terrorism, 1- 9, 11, 14, 17-18, 33, 36- 39, 42-44, 46, 56, 58-60, 62, 75-76, 79, 84, 87, 91-93, 95, 97, 106-107, 115-116, 118-119
Terrorism Prevention Reauthorization Act, 40
The Globe and Mail, 84, 121, 124, 129-130, 132-133
The Myth of Security at Canada's Airports, 89
Toronto Sun, 54, 126, 130, 134

Treaty of Washington, 76
Trudeau, Pierre E., 63

U

U.S. Customs and Immigration, 48
unilateralism, 32-33
United Nations, 1, 2, 17, 24, 33, 57, 63, 68, 80, 123-124
    Charter, 20, 22-23, 123
United Nations Security Council, 17-18, 20, 24-25, 29, 67, 76, 80, 123-124

V

Villepin, Dominique de, 33, 124

W

Walters, Barbara, 29
war, pre-emptive, 23
Wark, Wesley, 119-120, 129, 133
Washington Post, 98, 117, 126, 131, 133-134
Washington, George, 16, 122
Weber, Max, 2, 121
Welsh, Jennifer, 59, 89, 126, 129, 131
Whitaker, Reg, 60, 97, 127, 129, 131
White Paper, 65, 69-70, 75, 127-128
Wilson, Woodrow, 15, 125, 132
Wolfowitz, Paul, 22
Woolsey, James, 97, 131
World Trade Center, 1, 4, 8, 52, 57
World War II, 3, 12-13, 67, 72

Y

Yugoslavia, 68